SELF-CAT...
PORTUGAL

OTHER SELF-CATERING GUIDES PUBLISHED BY CROOM HELM

Self-catering in Spain, the Balearics and the Canary Islands
Carole Stewart with Chris Stewart

Self-catering in Greece, Mainland and Islands
Florica Kyriacopoulos and Tim Salmon

SELF-CATERING IN
PORTUGAL

Making the most of local food and drink

Carol Wright

CROOM HELM
London & Sydney

© 1986 Carol Wright
Croom Helm Publishers Ltd, Provident House, Burrell Row,
Beckenham, Kent BR3 1AT
Croom Helm Australia Pty Ltd, Suite 4, 6th Floor, 64-76 Kippax Street,
Surry Hills, NSW 2010, Australia

British Library Cataloguing in Publication Data

Wright, Carol
   Self-catering in Portugal: making the most of
   local food and drink.
   1. Food   2. Beverages   3. Cookery, Portuguese
   I. Title
   641'.09469   TX723.5/

   ISBN 0-7099-3663-X

Typeset in ITC Souvenir Light by
Leaper & Gard Ltd., Bristol, England
Printed and bound in Great Britain by
The Guernsey Press Co. Ltd., Guernsey, Channel Islands.

Contents

Acknowledgements

The author would like to thank the following people who have helped with the production of this book. In London: Jorge Felner da Costa, director, and João Custodio, deputy director, Portuguese National Tourist Office; Catarina de Camara, also of the PNTO; Ken Cook, British Airways; Tim Sandeman, George Sandeman & Co.; and Michael Geare (husband) for tea-making while the writing was going on. In Lisbon: Luis Cancella de Abreu, Direccao General do Turismo; Antonio Penha, director, Lisbon Hotel School; Mrs Filipa Vacondeus, food writer and TV food presenter; Lopo and Maria Emilia Cancella de Abreu, food and wine experts; Isabel Mello e Castro, public relations director, Lisbon Sheraton; and restaurant proprietor Michel da Costa.

1

Introduction: A PICTURE OF PORTUGAL

Portugal is still remote, cut off and less well known than most European countries. Separated from Spain and the rest of Europe by mountains and river valleys, this comparatively small, oblong country — roughly 350 miles long and 140 miles at its widest — looks out over its two Atlantic coasts to the sea.

Over the centuries, invaders have come to leave their mark on this proudly independent country. A thousand or more years BC, the Phoenicians came sailing up the Tagus to Lisbon. It is said their words *A Lis Ubo* — 'calm roadstead' — gave the capital its name (though in legend Lisbon is said to have been founded by Ulysses). Later, under Julius Caesar, the Romans came and called Lisbon 'Felicitas Julia'. They were followed by the Visigoths.

The Moors arrived around 911 and stayed until Lisbon was retaken in 1147. It was King Alfonso III (1248-79) who finally routed the remaining Moors from Portugal. But the Moors left behind cultural influences visible today in architectural features: the narrow streets of Alfama in Lisbon; the *azulejos*, blue and white tiles so characteristic of Portuguese houses inside and out; and the tall fretted and pierced chimneys of the Algarve.

Names starting with the prefix 'Al' are of Moorish origin and the Algarve perhaps retains most Moorish influence. The Moors brought to Portugal and Spain the oranges which remain a standard dessert, today usually peeled for the diner by the waiter and presented like an exotic flower on the plate. The Moors also planted almond groves and the almond from the Algarve forms the base of many sweetmeats of the area. Figs stuffed with roast almonds, cinnamon and sugar are served along with a glass of Madeira as an appetiser or dessert. There is a charming legend that tells of a northern princess married to a Moorish ruler of the Algarve who pined for winter snows in the warmth of the south. The ruler planted almond groves and their abundant blossom in late January is the 'snow' of the Algarve.

Chelb, now Silves, where until recently, they say, an Arabic dialect persisted, was the Moors' Algarve capital. It was then a more important river port than Lisbon. The name of this area, now Portugal's best known coast, means 'the land beyond'. Cut off from the rest of the country by high mountains, it remained unknown to the north. Portuguese monarchs after the twelfth century long signed themselves 'the kings of Portugal and the Algarve'.

The first military co-operation between Portugal and Britain came when English soldiers helped remove the Moors. Then, in 1385, the English helped the Portuguese defeat the Spanish at the battle of Aljubarrota, near Alcobaca in the central part of the country. A local sweetmeat (and the Portuguese are very fond of their sweetmeats) commemorates the battle. The pastry is made in the shape of a baker's wife who killed six Spaniards with a shovel when she found them hiding in her bread oven.

A more lasting memorial of that battle was the Treaty of Windsor, signed in 1386. This formally confirmed the Anglo-Portuguese alliance of 1373, which has lasted into the twentieth century. The alliance has been cemented over the centuries by exchange of princesses and port wine (known as the Englishman's drink) and latterly by tourism. English soldiers under the Duke of Wellington helped avert Napoleon's threatened domination of Portugal, defeating Massena, one of his generals, at the battle of Busaco in 1810. A small military museum nearby still contains mementoes of the campaign and the Duke of Wellington's family still bears a Portuguese title, that of the Marquis of Douro.

The Plantagenet princess, Philippa of Lancaster, married the Portuguese King John I in 1387. It was a happy marriage with several children given alternating English or Portuguese names. Their alliance (under which Anglo-Portuguese trade relations strengthened and, as in England, French became the language of the court) is touchingly recalled in the stone effigies on their tombs at the unfinished abbey at Batalha, which was partly designed by an English architect and built to commemorate the battle of Aljubarrota. Here the hands of the Portuguese prince and his English wife are shown to be eternally clasped.

Their son, the studious Henry, became known as the Navigator. He set in train events leading to Portugal, and much later Britain, becoming great colonists and explorers. Pre-occupied with the sea, Henry created fleets and set up a school of navigation at Sagres in the Algarve. He so fired the people with enthusiasm for his projects that the story goes that the citizens of Oporto slaughtered their cattle and sent the meat to provision the fleet; then, with winter coming, they realised they had nothing left but the entrails to eat. Ever since, tripe has been a popular dish in the Oporto area.

Until that time, it was believed that anyone leaving the westernmost point of Europe, the Cabo da Roca just north-west of Lisbon (also known as *fim del mundo*, the end of the world), would eventually fall off the edge of the earth. Henry's sailors didn't fall off, and, though Henry soon died, the Portuguese discovered two-thirds of the inhabited globe within a century and created sea routes to the Indies and the Orient. The names of the discoverers, commemorated in the powerful monument on the banks of the river Tagus at Lisbon, are world famous: Vasco da Gama, Magellan, Cabral (who discovered Brazil in 1510), Pedro Alves and Barto-lomeo Diaz. The greatest glory of this Age of Discovery came during the reign of Manoel I (1495-1521), when caravels would sail into Lisbon laden with gold, silks and spices. Lisbon was then the wealthy aristocrat of Europe, with palaces and churches — many later destroyed in the great earthquake of 1755 — and the banks of the Tagus were the site of one of Europe's largest shipbuilding yards.

The wonders that these early navigators brought to Portugal were enshrined for posterity in stone monuments in the style known as Manueline: barley sugar twisted columns, rope and anchor motifs and sea themes. The best example of the style can be seen in Belem on Lisbon's riverside. The sixteenth-century Jeronimos monastery, where Vasco da Gama is buried (whose discoveries and the subsequent tax on pepper enabled the church to be built), combines Gothic and Manueline features: ribbed columns like coral in an underground cave, rope, buckle and anchor adornments and tusked elephants supporting tomb covers.

Though Portugal's power was soon eclipsed by that of neighbouring Spain (who occupied Portugal from 1580 to 1640 when her colonies declined), the discoveries had brought ingredients that helped establish Portugal's cuisine. Vasco da Gama brought back curry spices from India in 1497 as preservatives and the use of turmeric and other curry flavours in thick fish stews is common, as well as saffron, also brought back by the discoverers. Cinnamon is commonly used in decorating and flavouring puddings.

Spain's influence on the food can perhaps be seen in small Gallician-style restaurants selling the *pudim* flan, an egg custard made sweeter and creamier in Portugal than it is in Spain. It came into the country with pilgrims visiting Compostella. Gaspacho and bread soups are common on both sides of the border.

After the Braganzas took the throne in 1640, the family remained monarchs of Portugal until 1910 when the country became a republic. About the time the Braganzas ascended the Portuguese throne, England was in the throes of a civil war which preoccupied her until the restoration of the monarchy in 1660. Charles II then married Catherine of Braganza, a quiet, convent-reared Portuguese princess to whom the king, in spite of his infidelities, remained remarkably devoted. As part of her dowry, Catherine brought Tangier and, more important, Bombay (which became Britain's first small foothold in the Indian sub-continent). Portugal continued to play a colonial role, retaining colonies in India (Goa), China (Macau), Africa (Mozambique and Angola) and South America (Brazil) into the twentieth century.

Catherine of Braganza was responsible for popularising tea drinking in England, giving it court approval, and today many Portuguese women continue to drink tea rather than coffee. However, Portugal offers some of the world's best coffee, brought in from Angola, Mozambique or Brazil. Some coffee shops offer up to 20 unblended types for the buyer to choose from and the smell of morning bean-roasting is characteristic of Lisbon. The creamy national dessert, egg custard, goes perfectly with coffee.

Catherine, according to some stories, also brought marmalade to England as a sea-sickness cure on her voyage over. The legend has probably arisen from confusion over the translation of the Portuguese word *marmelada*, which is quince perserve — thick, sweet and jelly-like and served sliced with cheese.

In the seventeenth century cinnamon and pepper, gifts of the Discoveries, were much in vogue, as well as chicken and the arrival of rice and potatoes. Before this time, I was told by Antonio Penha, a director of the Lisbon Hotel School and a keen collector of historical cook books, chestnuts (not potatoes) were the basis of Portuguese cooking.

With unlimited sugar from their colonies, the Portuguese developed a very sweet tooth. This is evident from the hundreds of local sweetmeats produced in almost every village and town all over the country. These are served in little paper cases or occasionally in small round earthenware dishes in tea and pastry shops; the customer pays his bill by counting the number of paper cases or dishes on the table. The visitor to the Algarve will come across intricate sweets made from almonds, figs, sugar and eggs in the pastry shops in Portimao, including the complicated Dom Rodrigues or 'thread eggs', bound together with cinnamon syrup and brown sugar (a wedding feast dish resembling a small bird's nest originating in Lagos).

Early in Portuguese history, the monasteries and abbeys developed the art of good living and lavish entertaining. It is worth going to see the kitchens of the twelfth-century abbey at Alcobaca, in the centre, which is the largest church in Portugal. The kitchens of the abbey are 90ft high and could feed 1,000 people. A stream for the freshest of fish runs through the kitchen and there are spit-roasting facilities for two oxen at a time and an eight-ton chopping block. A wealth of sweet dishes, spurred by the creations of the nuns in the late seventeenth and early eighteenth centuries, was made for visiting VIPs, and the recipes (many kept secret by the nuns) are still in use today. Names such as *Pasteis de Santa Clara* or *Ovos Moles* (soft eggs) *a Convento de Sao Miguel* give clues to their origin. One may find them on *pousada* menus.

Some rich, sweet, creamed concoctions have frugal bases of potatoes or *chila* (pumpkin) and some are flavoured with vinegar; an egg custard and caramel is made with bacon which gives it a deep, dark, rich flavour. The nuns were heavy-handed with eggs. Dozens of yolks were used in a pudding — and still are. Less coffee and chocolate are used, I was told, because of the expense. One restaurant in Lisbon, the Conventual, is run by women who make puddings to traditional recipes.

The custom of afternoon tea is a gentle, old-fashioned one in Portugal; people meet for dalliance, gossip or just a rest from shopping to savour a sweetmeat, sip their tea and watch the world go by. More substantial cakes are also made, such as the *bolo de miel* (honeycake) baked for Christmas in Madeira. The Madeira cake which we have copied is known on its island of origin as 'English' cake.

Portugal has become a popular tourist country, particularly the Algarve, originally discovered by the English who built villas there. Madeira, too was long used for warm winter acclimatisation by British expatriates on their way home from spells in the tropical outposts of the empire. Here for decades the word for a foreigner was simply 'English'. Nevertheless,

Portugal still seems a little remote and traditional, particularly in its cuisine which is among the least known to us with only one or two Portuguese restaurants in London.

The Portuguese, like the French, are devoted to their food and will drive long distances at weekends for a meal or to savour a special sweetmeat or to buy a local bread. They will call up restaurants to ensure a favourite dish is available, and they are fussy about the perfection of their ingredients, particularly fish. One restaurant, Muchaxo on the beach at Guincho near Lisbon, has its own 'lobster hospital' so lobsters reach the table as perfect as possible. At fishing ports like Nazare, where the Phoenician-style high-prowed boats are seen, daily *lota* or fish auctions are held at special markets, fish jetties or even on the beach with the best specimens displayed on pedestals of sand; fresh fish is carried inland in little vans. In Lisbon, though the custom is almost dead, sturdy women known as *varinhas*, with a Cockney-like sense of humour, still carry basket-loads of fresh fish through the streets calling out their wares for housewives to buy.

The sea and its produce dominate Portuguese food. Seafood, from lobsters to *perceves* (little barnacles), is eaten. There is plenty of sole, hake, halibut, mullet and sea bass. Tuna is caught off the Algarve coast in May and June, when the sea runs dark purple with the fishes' blood. In Madeira, the *espada*, a yard-long black and white blotched fish only found here or off Japan, is eaten, sometimes with bananas. Swordfish is also popular from south of Lisbon, at Setubal, and Lisboans cross the Tagus to little fish restaurants at Cacilhas which specialise in sole, while looking lovingly across the river to the seven-hilled horizon of their city.

With this wealth of fresh fish, it is surprising that the national dish, eaten all over the country, is salted, dried cod known as *bacalhau*. Every year for 400 years past, the fishermen have gone away for six months across the Atlantic to the Grand Banks off Newfoundland and fished for cod. The cod is brought back, salted, sun-dried and sold in flat, cardboard-like portions that need careful pre-preparation to make into the many different recipes served in Portugal.

Sardines are perhaps the second best-known Portuguese fish and one of the country's main food exports, with Marie Elisabeth, a brand well known in Britain. Fresh sardines are cheap in summer, bigger and richer than those we get in cans and perfect barbecue or beach-restaurant food.

The influence of the sea and sailors is reflected in the *fado. Fado* means fate, and fate is Portugal, one will be told. *Fado* found in Lisbon (with a more romantic version sung by the students of the university city of Coimbra) is a sad, haunting song best sung deep-throated with what is known as a 'wine voice'. Said to be the song of the sixteenth-century sailors of the Discoveries, the *fado* is a song of parting, love and sadness. Today it is often sung by women dressed in traditional clothes topped by a black shawl, leaning against a wall, and accompanied by Portuguese and Spanish guitars. The origin may be Moorish and the best time to hear *fado* is on a summer night when singers perform on the street corners of the stepped alleys of Lisbon's Alfama district, though the purists still think the best place to listen to *fado* is on the water. One of the most haunting *fados* I have heard was sung by Goanese boys on the beach as the sun fizzed down into the Indian Ocean.

This sad introspection and fatalism and Atlantic outlook of Portugal is less easily understood than the Latin *joie de vivre* of other countries. Yet the Latin streak is there — manifest in a love of fiesta, the proud show-off of the male, gambling, fast driving and macho bullfighting (even if the bull is not actually killed in the ring). There are bull dancer teams of men who bravely somersault over the bull's back and wrestle him to a standstill, rather as they did in ancient Crete. The fire is tempered by the country and climate.

The north of Portugal, the Douro, along the border with Spain, is harsh and the mountains of the north-west bleak and chill in winter. Yet, where the land is painstakingly terraced, there grow the grapes for the rich, sweet port wine. Here, as in many parts of Portugal, traditional religious festivals persist and older customs of pagan origin in which the pig and phallic worship are much involved. At Amirantes, the local cake is made in phallic shapes and called *foguetes* (rockets). At Viana, on the coast, for the patron saint's day men and women give each other bread shaped with explicitly sexual detail and the *azulejos* tiles in the church have a very carnal theme. Every town and village has its *romaries*, or religious pilgrimage, procession and fair. Further south, one of the most elaborate is the tray festival (*tabuleiro*) at Tomar, where girls carry a crown head-dress as tall as themselves made from loaves and ears of wheat.

Feasts are a relaxation and, on the pilgrimage, sustaining stews are carried. *Cozidos* or stews are food for warmth — simple foods of the people, in which meats can be mixed as available and enriched with spices, herbs and vegetables. Widely used flavourings are fresh coriander leaves, lemon juice — also used with meat — and meat is often cooked in wine or with Port or Madeira. The Minho in the north has the

13

country's highest rainfall and produces plentiful fruit and vegetables; it is also where the lamprey is still eaten. To the east, the drier plains of the Alentejo produce wheat rather than vegetables so a dry bread soup (açorda) is the characteristic fare. Olives, sheep and cork are the other produce of this area and pigs which feed off the cork oak acorns. The cork is used to line a carrier for soups, hot or cold according to season, carried to the fields by agricultural workers for their lunch.

Since the revolution of the 1970s the tradition of maids and private house cooks has much declined. The younger women, not knowing how to cook in the traditional ways, have taken to preparing lighter, faster and simpler dishes for the home; the preservation and production of traditional recipes is now enshrined in the restaurants. At home housewives are developing lighter ways of cooking with less olive oil, and using cheaper margarine or vegetable oils instead; there is also more use of vegetables, pasta, chicken, and yoghurt. TV programmes showing how to make traditional dishes have a big following. With a change in diet, the Portuguese are becoming taller and bigger. Female chefs are still found in the restaurants, and along the coast there is a tradition of the fisherman's wife running a small restaurant while her husband is at sea. Small and dark, these are often excellent restaurants where the women cheerfully bustle round cooking in big earthenware platters on top of the stove.

There is only one place that can be called a health farm, in the north of the country, near Lamego. Throughout Portugal, however, there is increased emphasis on lighter foods, with quality not quantity now the criterion. The spicier influence of Indian cuisine and Mozambique African flavours are becoming more evident. There are now about five Indian restaurants in Lisbon.

Nouvelle cuisine is somewhat alien to the Portuguese, but there are one or two establishments in Lisbon, notably Chef Silva and Michel Costa, which practise it. Portuguese who have travelled may have a Bocuse book and try a few recipes at home. Michel's menu includes hors d'oeuvres like rabbit terrine with prunes and Cumberland sauce, or blinis with smoked swordfish with lemon cream. Sole is cooked in dry port and served on a bed of fresh spinach mousse; a crusty country loaf will be stuffed with a mousse of bacalhau (dried cod) flavoured with port wine.

For the visitor, the government has helped keep alive decorative and culinary themes in the pousadas (a word literally meaning 'to perch'). These are government-run hotels, often in restored castles, palaces or forts originally set up for motorists to see out-of-the-way but scenically or historically worthwhile places. *Pousadas* of note include Obidos, the honeymoon gift town of kings of Portugal to their queens; a convent at Evora; Santa Reina Isabel, a queen's home at Estremoz; the Duke of Palmela's castle at Palmela; a sunny farmhouse in the Algarve; and alpine structures in the northern mountains. The food is regional and traditional. Portuguese recipes are highlighted on the menus and annual cooking competitions are held. A newer idea to find out more about lifestyles in Portugal is the opening up of private manor houses to paying guests, often on a bed and breakfast basis, but in some cases visitors can dine with the owners; or there are self-catering apartments and cottages for rent where one can shop for food and prepare meals.

Time-honoured ingredients are not easily replaced by convenience foods. Portugal is the world's fourth olive oil producer but it has become expensive and vegetable oil is now increasingly used for cooking, while countrywomen cling to the use of white pig's fat for cooking. Fresh fish is preferred to fish fingers or frozen portions and even cooking pots are traditional; the *cataplana*, or metal steamer, of the Algarve is perhaps used more in restaurants than homes, although it is sold in many places, along with inexpensive and practical earthenware platters and pots.

Recipes, of course, reflect the regions. In the north, where the tall-stemmed couve cabbage grows round each cottage, there are thick nourishing vegetable soups such as *caldo verde* (cabbage soup), which has become a national staple. In the east, in the wheatlands of the Alentejo, the soups are based on bread, often just with garlic and water, or with game and meat. On the coast, fish soups and stews are flavoured with herbs and spices. The classic cuisine term 'in the Portuguese way' means with a sauce of onions, tomatoes and garlic cooked in olive oil. While herds of Aberdeen Angus and other British breeding stock are being reared and fine quality beef is available, pork is more usual in the north, with plentiful spiced sausages and hams. At Mealhada, roast sucking pig is the speciality, sold in pink juicy hunks edged with spices and herbs on crusty bread from stalls and restaurants in the little town. Chicken is also a national meat and the cock is the national symbol of Portugal. Game from heath and headlands and lamb from the Alentejo is available and in certain areas there is a liking for offal — liver in Lisbon, for instance, and tripe in Oporto.

Though the Portuguese have a sweet tooth they have few

cheeses and do not have a large number of varied puddings and desserts. In fact, to the casual *eye*, it seems the only alternative are fresh oranges, or seasonal fruit, or *pudim* flan. The *pudim* flan, the creamy egg custard, is also known as 365 after the number of days in the year when it, like *bacalhau*, will be offered on restaurant menus.

The recipe variations sound like something from Mrs Beeton. 'Take a dozen eggs' is the basis of many such puddings. Often these puddings are served mid-afternoon with a cup of tea instead of after a meal. The Portuguese allow a little humour in their cookery terms. There's *pao constipado*: 'bread with a cold' and some of the puddings have lovely, slightly naughty, names. Angel's Breasts (*papas d'anjou*) was once translated for me as 'titbits'; or Nun's Tummies is another custard creation made in small cake moulds from egg yolks, flavoured with lemon and soaked after cooking in syrup. *Bolas de Sao Goncalo* (the saint of marriage) is the aptly named sweetmeat of Amirantes (the name of the northern town meaning 'lovers').

A good *pudim* flan will be rich and creamy — a soft egg custard cooked in lemon syrup perhaps. *Sonhos* (dreams) is another nationally popular sweet of sweetened egg mixture deep fried till light and puffy and served sprinkled with sugar and cinnamon or with a light sugar syrup flavoured with cinnamon or lemon. A very sweet egg dish, originating from Aveiro but found nationally, is *Ovos Moles* (soft eggs). The mix allows roughly an ounce of sugar per egg and three egg yolks per person, bound to a paste with sweet white wine and thickened over a gentle heat. Chilled before serving, the sweetmeats are served on Chantilly cream topped with finely chopped almonds cooked in caramel sauce. The mixture can also be used as a sauce or to fill a *mille-feuille* pastry tart. It is a fine partner to tangy, soft fruits like raspberries. An old Portuguese custom was to decorate the dish of *Ovos Moles* with cinnamon, forming the initial of the principal guest.

And, at the end of a good meal, the Portuguese mark of appreciation is the thumb and forefinger gently encircling the ear-lobe and a little expressive sigh through pursed lips.

2
USING THIS BOOK

This book is intended to help the holidaymaker in a self-catering apartment or villa in Portugal to make the most of fresh local ingredients found in holiday areas. The recipes in later chapters use ingredients that are easily found in the daily markets held in villages, fishing ports, cities and even along the roadsides. Many of the recipes are for traditional Portuguese dishes, slightly adapted to make them simpler or quicker to make.

The recipes have been set out in metric and imperial measures and in making them up one should stick to one set or the other. Recipes in this book are calculated on the basis of 25 grams to the ounce. Portugal, of course, uses metric measures — a fact to remember when shopping. Another point to remember is that Portugal's unit of currency, the *escudo*, is printed like a US dollar sign, which can be confusing.

Portuguese recipes can, of course, be taken home as happy holiday memories. Most of the ingredients are easily available in your local grocery or supermarket.

To help at home or on holiday, here are a few preparation and cookery hints for cooking the Portuguese way. *Bacalhau*, the dried, salted cod, can be found in Italian (*baccalo*) and Spanish (*bacalao*) groceries and in West Indian stores. It looks like pieces of stiff, grey cardboard and should be kept in a cool, dry place, well wrapped and separated from other foods to which it might impart flavour. *Bacalhau* should be soaked for at least 24 hours if thin; thicker pieces need 48 hours. Cover the dried fish with plain, cold water and change this water once or twice during the soaking period. When cooking, boil gently till quite soft, which takes about 2-3 hours. Many *bacalhau* recipes are basically boiled cod and potatoes mixed with a cheese sauce and baked in the oven.

A simple *bacalhau* dish to try is *Bacalhau a Bras*. Cut well soaked and desalted cod into small pieces. Take twice as many potatoes as the amount of fish, slicing them long and thin to be fried like chips. Chop some onions to taste. Pour some olive oil into a frying pan, and one crushed clove of garlic (remove when browned), fry cod, add potatoes, mix well. When cooked, add well-beaten eggs (allowing 3 eggs per serving). Take care not to overcook the mixture.

Sardines freshly grilled are quite different from the tiny, oily, mushy ones that come in tins. Fresh sardines are occasionally available from good fishmongers and supermarkets. Frozen sardines are also imported from Portugal. Tinned sardines, well drained, can be used for grilling, in hors d'oeuvres and in made up dishes.

Adding the vital tasty slice of sausage to a soup, instead of the unobtainable Portuguese sausage, use Italian, French or German blood sausage cut into small pieces. Garlic sausage can be substituted for *chourico*.

The most popular flavouring in Portugal is fresh coriander (*coentro*). This can be bought occasionally at home from better greengrocers and specialist shops, but a strong herb like basil can be used instead, though the flavour is substantially different. Portuguese parsley is stronger than our own. In making the *caldo verde* soup, the characteristic *couve* cabbage of northern Portugal can be replaced by finely shredded kale or dark green cabbage.

Colorau is a ground spice of peppers used in many dishes. There is no real equivalent here but cayenne or paprika could be used instead. The *piri piri* sauce which goes so well with grilled chicken in the Algarve can be made at home. Take off the top of each of a handful of chillies before placing them in ½ pint (¼ litre) of olive oil. Add a crushed bay leaf and grated lemon rind and leave to infuse for several hours at the bottom of the oven at the lowest possible heat or on top of the stove. Bottle and store. This sauce can be brushed on chicken, pork or shellfish before grilling.

Tomato puree can be used in recipes instead of fresh-cooked tomatoes. A tomato sauce used for cooking fish in an oven-proof dish can be made by frying one finely chopped onion and half a crushed garlic clove in two tablespoons (30ml) of olive oil in a thick pan (do not allow to become brown). Add one tin of chopped, peeled tomatoes, salt, pepper and a bay leaf. Simmer uncovered for an hour. Add water to taste, heat and use as a sauce.

A green pepper paste is much used in the Alentejo region as a method of preserving peppers out of season; or a thick pulp of fresh peppers can be used instead to spread over meat. To make a paste to store, pound or liquidise together de-seeded peppers with a little ginger, chopped onion, and salt. Put ingredients in a jar and cover with olive oil. Store before using to improve the flavour.

Refogado is a term which occurs in many Portuguese recipes. It is an onion puree, the basis of many dishes, including thick soups and *bacalhau* recipes and also a garnishing sauce for meat or fish. A basic *refogado* is made by cooking a finely chopped onion to a pulp in a frying pan with one tablespoon (15ml) of olive oil. Cover the pan to keep the onion soft. Tinned or sieved tomatoes can be added. Add salt and pepper to taste. Garlic or bay leaf may be added according to the type of flavouring needed.

Rice is easily cooked the Portuguese way and is useful for making non quality grains more succulent (see page 39). Melt butter or use olive oil in a pan. Mix dry rice in a pan till evenly coated over a low heat. Add twice the quantity of water as rice. Cover the pan and boil for 20 minutes on a low heat. The rice will absorb all the moisture and the grains will be separated and fluffy.

A sugar thermometer will be of help in creating the many types of syrup used in Portuguese puddings. To go with the ubiquitous egg pudding, a caramel sauce can be made using 3oz (75 grams) of sugar to $\frac{1}{8}$ pint (75ml) of water. Heat together and stir till boiling. Continue to boil without stirring until it is golden brown. Pour into a warm mould. A Portuguese *pousada* way — ideal for quick results — is to scatter granulated sugar on the bottom of a wide frying pan, cook till it burns, pour on a little boiling water and mix well. Or, another way, told me by a skilled Portuguese cook, is to boil sugar and water in a pan until the sugar is burnt and dark. Pour over a little cold water, mix and use to coat the inside of a mould. To make an egg pudding to go in the mould, this same cook suggested beating six whole eggs with six dessert spoons (a popular Portuguese measure) of sugar and a large teacup of milk. Beat until well mixed and place in the mould. Cook till firm in a *bain marie*, which takes about 20 minutes.

As well as helping you to enjoy Portugal's characteristic cuisine, this book shows you how to find the various foods in the markets and shops, what the local specialities are, what common cooking utensils are found in Portugal and how they should be used. Eating out is covered in a separate chapter, so the holiday cook need not be tied to preparing every meal, especially when local restaurants are very reasonably priced. There are some notes on the leading wines so that you can enjoy new tastes with the recipes and indications of what foods they go best with. The bibliography details some more books to read before, during or after your holiday.

The recipe sections aim to provide a flavour of your holiday surroundings coupled with ease of preparation and cooking with minimal equipment. Breakfast on a Portuguese holiday can be light and local, with coffee, fresh bread, quince preserve and fresh peaches or other fruit; lunch, simple grilled fish or a big fresh salad and fruits. Dinner, when sightseeing and sun possibilities are over for the day, should be the main meal at which to try out some of the recipes in this book.

PUBLIC HOLIDAYS IN PORTUGAL

The following are some days to note when shops, banks and other public facilities are closed:

January 1 — New Year's Day
February — Shrove Tuesday (varies each year)
April — Good Friday
April 25 — Day of the Revolution
May 1 — Labour Day
June 10 — Camoes Day (a famous Portuguese poet)
June — Corpus Christi
August 15 — The Assumption
October 5 — Day of the Republic
November 1 — All Saints' Day
December 1 — Independence Day
December 8 — Feast of the Immaculate Conception
December 25 — Christmas Day

TRAVEL INFORMATION

Portuguese National Tourist Office, New Bond Street House, 1-5 New Bond Street, London W1Y 0NP (tel: 01-493 3873)
Portuguese National Tourist Office, 548 Fifth Avenue, New York, NY 10036 (tel: 212-354 4403)

3

LOCAL FRUIT AND VEGETABLES

From the harsh mountains of the Douro in the north to the gentle warmth of the southern Algarve, the varied climate of Portugal produces a diverse selection of fruits. Oranges are grown virtually all over the country. From the north come apples, plums and grapes; from the south, pomegranates, figs, chestnuts, melons, and peaches; from the central southern and eastern region, olives. Portugal's Atlantic islands produce fruits like bananas and pineapples. Easy to serve for desserts, the fruits most commonly available are listed below:

Bananas (*bananas*) come from Madeira and the Cape Verde islands and are also grown in the Algarve. A hand of bananas hanging outside a small shop often indicates a fruitseller (*fruitaria*). Another much used fruit sign is the pineapple.

Cherries (*cereja*) also come from the Monchique area. These are served locally mixed with oranges and soaked in Alphonso 111 wine.

Chestnuts (*castanhas*), grown in the mountains of Monchique in the Algarve, feature in restaurant dishes served in the region.

Chestnuts

Custard apple (*anona*) is a Portuguese fruit from Madeira, shaped like a large green hand grenade and served in Lisbon restaurants in the spring. It has creamy flesh rather like a

21

Custard apple

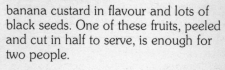

banana custard in flavour and lots of black seeds. One of these fruits, peeled and cut in half to serve, is enough for two people.

Figs (*figos*) are a speciality of the Algarve. These are often served, stuffed with roast almonds, as an accompaniment to drinks before or after a meal.

Grapefruit (*toranja*) are available all over Portugal.

Grapes (*uvas*) are grown all over the country and also come from Madeira.

Figs

Lemons (*limao*) are grown in all parts of Portugal, even the inhospitable seeming lands of the Douro. Commonly a wedge of lemon is served with meats such as pork or lamb cutlets, as well as with fish.

Medlars (*nesperas*) are found towards the end of the year and are eaten while still firm and juicy but not bletted (left to rot and become soft) as in Britain.

Melon (*melao*) is delicious cut in half and soaked with a little white or red port or with a little sweet Madeira wine poured in the seed cavity. Water-melons are grown in the Algarve.

Medlars

Oranges (*laranja*) were introduced to Portugal by the Moors, though some say they came to Lisbon in the 1630s from

China and then spread to other parts of Europe. Oranges are Portugal's most commonly eaten fruit, available year-round. Bitter oranges are found around the Setubal area, south of Lisbon, and made into a sticky sweet preserve with liqueur. Oranges are used to flavour cakes and are served in restaurants, ready peeled and fanned out into segments like a flower. Or, a wedge of orange is often served with meat, particularly pork. The sweet juicy seedless navel oranges are the best.

Peaches (*pessego*) are grown in the Algarve.

Pears (*pera*) come from the north of Portugal and are delicious poached in red wine.

Pineapples (*ananas*) are grown on the island of S. Miguel in the Azores and sold seasonally in mainland Portugal. The pineapples are small and sweet and cost around 340 *escudos* each.

Plums (*ameixas*) are grown in the more northerly areas. The plums of Elvas in the east are well known — sugared and sold in boxes, especially around Christmas time.

Pomegranates (*romas*) ripen in the Algarve in late summer. They are big and golden and contain many seeds.

Tangerines (*mexirica*) are grown in many parts of the country.

Pomegranates

Tangerines

Vegetables are grown in the north, often intercropped between the vines. Or, in the Minho, the tall-stemmed *couve* cabbage is grown in phalanxes around houses as a fencing. It is carried to market in great bundles by the women who, from a distance, look like walking cabbage plants. In the Algarve, the 'garden of Portugal' with its rich soil, many vegetables and even some sugar cane are grown as well as rice.

Portuguese vegetables are generally similar to those familiar to us in the UK but they are served in different ways. Meat and two vegetables is not usual in Portugal. Pommes frites (chips) is the ubiquitous garnish, or sometimes salad. Rice is often mixed with vegetables and herbs as an alternative to plain vegetables.

Asparagus (*aspargos*) is grown in the Algarve, ripening earlier than in the UK.

Avocados (*pera abacare*) are grown in Madeira and shipped to the mainland.

Broad beans (*favas*) are popular with country people living around Lisbon who make them into a main dish with coriander, onion, chopped bacon, sliced sausage and meat broth stewed in a covered pot.

French beans (*feijao verde*) are grown especially around Lisbon. Whole French beans, deep fried, are charmingly known as 'garden fish' (*peixinhos da horta*). These are cooked in deep fat, in a wine batter coating, and eaten with the fingers. Beans are often served with tomatoes and onions.

Asparagus

Cabbage (*couve*) is a staple of northern Portugal. It is shredded very thinly to make the national soup dish of *caldo verde* (see page 73), served with a slice of local sausage in it. Deep bluish green with a long stem, the cabbage is shredded so fine with special cutters that it is hardly cooked at all. In markets one can buy *couve* ready shredded.

Cauliflowers (*couve flor*) grown in the Algarve are so massive that they easily do for four meals. Cauliflower is often used to make a pie filling for family suppers.

Coriander (*coentro*): the fresh leaves are sold in bunches in markets, little grocery shops and supermarkets. It is chopped up to flavour dishes of all kinds.

Lettuce (*alface*) is often used as a salad accompaniment to liver (*iscas*) in the Lisbon area.

Onions (*cebolas*) are an absolute 'must' in Portuguese cooking, along with tomatoes and garlic. Grown everywhere, they are usually big and full of flavour.

Peas (*ervilhas*) are another vegetable popular in the Lisbon area where they are cooked long and slowly with smoked pork, salami-style sausage (or any smoked meat or sausage) or lean boiling bacon. This mixture, with the addition of a poached egg, makes a good and simple supper dish. *Ervilhas tortas* may be seen on menus. This is mange tout — cut across in thick pieces and served with other vegetables in a rice accompaniment to meat and fish.

Potatoes (*batatas*): chips are popular everywhere and served in *tasca*-style small restaurants with meat dishes in earthenware containers. Potatoes are mashed into soups, boiled with fish, and fried with meat; and they are often mixed with dried cod. Both ordinary and sweet potatoes are grown in the Algarve. Usually potatoes are cooked Irish style, with their skins removed after cooking. A waxy type of potato is best for this treatment.

Spinach (*espinafres*) is popular in the

Avocados

Coriander

central part of the country. In Lisbon, it can be served pureed as the base of a chick pea and bacon mixture or as a base for sole, plainly grilled. Again with chick peas, spinach is served with *bacalhau*.

Tomatoes

Tomatoes (*tomate*) — large, misshapen and slightly green — are beloved all over Portugal and used in the basic '*à la Portuguaise*' sauce with onions and garlic. Tomatoes are used in great abundance in the Algarve and made into chutneys and purees by local factories. Boiled potatoes are served with tomato sauce and tomato sauce is much used as an accompaniment for eggs, meat or fish and as an omelette filling.

Turnips (*nabos*): the tops rather than the root are used.

In markets, mixed salad greens are sold in little packets and bags, combined often with appropriate herbs and watercress, and this saves a lot of preparation. The shredded *couve* cabbage for *caldo verde* soup can be found in packets in markets and supermarkets. In the top Lisbon food shop, Jeronimos e Martins, a packet of *caldo verde* pieces was 21 *escudos*. In supermarkets such as Celeiro in Lisbon one can find cabinets of frozen vegetables such as the Ross brand imported from Belgium.

4

MEATS, POULTRY AND FISH

Cuts of meat are always a problem for the shopper abroad. Tiny, bare-looking meat shops and market stalls are the best sources, though meat is rarely hung long enough. In Portugal the cuts (see Glossary p. 123) are more akin to those seen in America than in Britain. Lists of cuts and grades are often not well displayed in shops.

For veal and pork for most Portuguese-style recipes it is best to buy a boned leg. The *lombo* of pork much used in Portugal is the fillet, though in Britain the grain is different. Ask for a big fillet. Steak is rare and *bifes* is often from a cow. Chicken and pork are the most common meats and many warming stews of the north are made from whole chickens with pigs' tails, trotters and pieces of sausage added to make the dish more substantial and nourishing.

Beef (*vaca*) Aberdeen Angus herds are established in the Minho area and the quality of Portuguese beef has been much improved through cross-breeding with imported stock, but it may still seem tough to the alien palate. *Rosbife* is around 1300 *escudos* a kilo and *vaca* (more literally from a cow) is about 950 *escudos* a kilo. *Bife a frigideira* is a common way of cooking a steak and easy to copy for simple self-catering meals. The steak is cooked on top of the stove in little round earthenware dishes with an onion sauce and finally topped with a poached egg (see also page 67).

Chicken (*frango*) is common and much used in all kinds of dishes. If buying near the coast, check that the bird has not been reared on fish meal, which can give it a rank, fishy taste. Chickens are obtainable from supermarkets ready prepared for the table. In Oporto there are many small restaurants for *frango no forno*, where chicken is roasted in old brandy or port. Another traditional dish is chicken in the pot (*frango na pucara*), for which deep decorated earthenware casseroles are used. The chicken is sealed in the casserole and cooked with ham, mustard, brandy, port and seasoning.

Duck (*pato* or wild duck, *pato bravo*) is best bought from September to February and is often served with huge bowls of vegetable rice.

Game (*caça*): most easily obtainable is partridge from the area around Lisbon and rabbit and quail from the Algarve headlands. Rabbit is a popular meat in the Algarve and rabbit paté with prunes is often seen on menus.

Hams: the best smoked mountain-style hams come from Lamego and Chaves in the north. Buying a ham by the leg is expensive — around 6700 *escudos*. Salty morsels of ham are served before meals with pieces of pickled vegetable. *Presunto* is a fine quality cured ham from the leg of pork and resembles the Italian *prosciutto*. *Paio* is a smoked pork loin meat. *Salpicao* is smoked loin of pork with spices. *Toucinho* is the belly of pork similar to bacon which can be used to flavour various dishes.

Kid (*cabrito*) is usually served as a roast.

Lamb (*anho*, *borrego*) mostly comes from the Alentejo area but is little used for

Presunto (ham)

28

meat as the animals are kept for their wool. What lamb there is comes mainly in the form of leg and chop cuts. The price is about 700 *escudos* a kilo.

Offal (*sobras, sobejos*): tripe hanging up looking like wrinkled oilskins is a common sight in and around Oporto. It can be cooked in rolls around chopped bacon, pepper, parsley and onion filling, in salted water with herbs and coriander and a bay leaf for 3 to 4 hours (or pressure cooked for one hour) tripe cooked this way is served with a spicey sauce. In the Oporto area tripe is also cooked with haricot beans and smoked sausage. In Lisbon, *iscas* (thinly sliced liver) is marinated in white wine and herbs and then fried with ham. Or, thinly sliced onions, potatoes and garlic are mixed together in a bowl with salt, pepper and a bay leaf and cooked in butter or pork fat till golden; then liver and a little wine are added and the meat and vegetables are served over boiled potatoes.

Suckling pig

Pork (*porco*) is a national meat found especially in the north. Suckling pig, pink and juicy with a slab of bread and a glass of wine, is the custom at Mealhada, north of Lisbon. In the Algarve, pork is mixed with clams, white wine, herbs and onions and steamed in a *cataplana* (see page 61). Portuguese pork is fattier than that sold here. In the past it was always free range but, according to Portuguese food critics, this is less often the case today and so the meat is less tasty.

Sausages: *chourico* is a crude sausage made of cured pork pepped up with garlic and paprika. About seven inches long and an inch in diameter, it is sliced into soups and stews for extra flavour. *Murcela* is a blood sausage from the north used in *caldo verde* soup. It is made with pork, pork blood and spices. *Linguica* is similar to *chourico* but thinner and usually seasoned with paprika. Often in restaurants little earthenware barbecues (many in the shape of pigs or boats) are brought to the table so the sausages can be flamed in brandy before being eaten with bread. *Alheira* is a fresh sausage made from pork, poultry or game. *Farinheira*, from the Alentejo, is a smoked sausage made from fat pork, wheat flour and seasoning.

Chourico

SEAFOOD

Fishing has been the mainstay of the Portuguese diet since Phoenician times and a visit to Nazare, a major fishing port on the west coast, shows the high-prowed, Phoenician-style boats, decorated with a protective eye symbol, still in use today. The *lota*, or daily fish auctions, are held on the beach when the catch comes in and are best seen at places such as Sesimbra, south of Lisbon, and Portimao in the Algarve. Cascais, near Lisbon, is unusual in having an evening *lota* in the fish auction hall where restaurateurs and market buyers go to bid for boxes of fresh fish.

Most fish in Portugal is sold fresh, even inland. But frozen fish is increasing in supermarkets much to the disgust of purists who suspect that unbranded packs sold in smaller coastal areas contain unsold fresh fish which has been chopped up and frozen. Findus and Igloo are good reliable frozen brands. Fish is widely used in thick soups (well spiced) and stews. Often in the markets piles of fish heads are seen for those who can only afford a little to make a fish stew. It is best to buy fish in the markets held most mornings in the major communities. The fish is usually sold in a separate building by sturdy women. Long used to English-language shoppers, market women in the Algarve and Lisbon areas usually know the English names of fish, although some species are not found elsewhere. Sea fish are available all year round in Portugal. Exceptions are sardines, which are at their best after June; squid which is good in late spring; and *savel* (shad) and lamprey available in winter.

Clams

Clams (*ameijoas*) are more akin to our cockles. Small, fan-shaped light shells about half an inch across, they are used in the Algarvean *cataplana* dish, cooked with pork, herbs, onions and wine, or to make a soup in the Lisbon area. Big packs of clams, somewhat gritty, can be bought at supermarkets as a substitute for more expensive shrimps in a prawn cocktail dish.

Dried Cod (*bacalhau*), see also page 17) should be in the grocery section for it is sold dried like cardboard in flat pieces or sheets which are hoisted by strings to the ceiling. It must be well soaked before use. It is best to try out some of the many *bacalhau* dishes in restaurants to acquire the taste before making any recipes yourself. The cod is fished off Newfoundland, with the fishermen using little row-boats from the mother ship. It is still a risky business and fishermen's wives often put on black shawls of mourning when the boats leave, wearing them till their men return safe. Originally the dried cod was a way of keeping the catch through the winter. The cod is dried in the sun around Aveiro, where salt is also produced. The salted cod kept Henry the Navigator's sailors going on long voyages

and it is now the national dish of Portugal.
Every day some *bacalhau* variation is
served in restaurants, but *the* day for such
fish dishes is Friday. It is not a cheap food
(about 847 *escudos* for 1.650 kg), but it
contains three times the food value as the
same weight of fresh fish. With visitors
one of the most popular ways of serving
bacalhau is in *pasteis* form: the cod,
mixed with potatoes, is dropped in
spoonfuls into hot fat and deep fried until
it is light and fluffy.

Crab (*caranguejo*); big crabs are found
around Cascais and spider crabs (*santola*)
are common. These are served cold with
egg yolk, mustard and lemon sauce or
spiced and baked hot in their shells. Crab
costs from 700 *escudos* per kilo at the
market.

Hake (*pescada*) is more common in
Lisbon. The delicate flesh can be used in
several ways, and it is lean and suitable for
dieters, containing only 74 calories per
100 grams.

Halibut (*cherne*) is popular in Lisbon.

Lamprey

Lamprey (*lampreia*) is in season in
spring. An ugly primitive creature once
favoured by royals in England, it is fished
in the rivers of northern Portugal and
casseroled in red wine.

Lobster (*lagosta*) found around Sagres
in the Algarve and round Lisbon, is

expensive: current market prices range from 3000-4000 *escudos* per kilo. Also occasionally available are *bruxas* (witches) — tiny, prawn-sized lobsters.

Mackerel (*carapau*) is usually marinated in an *escabeche* sauce (see page 36), in the same way as tuna, and eaten as an hors d'oeuvre. Like sardines it is very cheap.

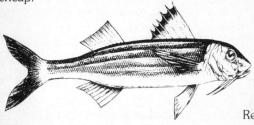

Red mullet

Mullet (*salmonetes*) is available in red and grey types.

Oysters (*ostras*) come mainly from Quarteira in the Algarve and Troia to the south of Lisbon.

Perceves is an unusual barnacle often found at beach restaurants in the Guincho area near Lisbon. It is about a quarter of an inch across and purplish in colour. When cooked, the flesh is soft and tastes of the sea and iodine.

Prawns (*gambas*) are big and excellent but expensive — from 700 to 2300 *escudos* per kilo. These are especially found around Monte Gordo in the Algarve and in Lisbon. Many restaurants have tempting displays of prawns as hors d'oeuvres.

Sardines (*sardinhas*) are probably a better known fish from Portugal than cod, but, in its native setting, this fish seems unrelated to the tiny tinned sardines we buy here as exports from Portugal. Fresh sardines, available locally from June to October, are about six inches long, silvery blue and very cheap (50-100 *escudos* per kilo). Sardines are also sold ready cooked from stalls for the June festival in Lisbon.

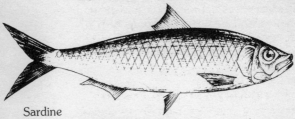

Sardine

In the Algarve and other coastal areas, sardines barbecued simply at beachside restaurants, make a perfect casual meal with crusty bread, salad and a bottle of chilled *vinho verde*. Sometimes sardines are cooked in a bread dough case with chopped onions. These fish are so rich in their own oils that they are usually just grilled with herbs and the juices allowed to seep into rounds of bread; they are eaten flavoured only with a little salt. When cleaned, the smaller sardines can be stuffed with a bunch of mint and cooked; the larger ones can be split open for grilling sprinkled with herbs. In Sesimbra a sardine stew is made with whole sardines minus head and guts, potatoes, onions, tomatoes, pepper and a little water. Chop sardines after the water has boiled and cook on a low heat for about 15 minutes shaking the pan occasionally.

Scabbard fish

Scabbard fish (*peixe espada*) is seen in the markets, stretched out, a yard long with pointed thin snout and silvery scales.

Sea bass (*robalo*) is another popular fish seen on restaurant menus and in the markets. *Robalinhos* in spring are mini versions of this fish — sardine-sized and served grilled — but are fiddly to eat with small bones.

Sole (*linguado*) is usually served grilled plain with spinach. Stuffed sole is a typical dish of the Algarve.

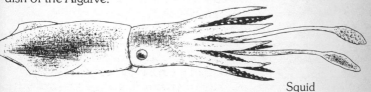

Squid

Squid (*lulas*) is found more towards the southern half of Portugal, along with octopus. Squid is usually served stuffed and costs about 24 *escudos* in the supermarket. One Lisbon housewife told me she cooked squid by taking the head off, cleaning the inside, washing it well and stewing pieces in a small pan. She makes a *refogado* with pepper to taste, then, using this to stuff the squid closes it up with a toothpick. A second *refogado* sauce is made with plenty of tomato pulp, pepper and *piri piri* sauce (see page 18). The squid is cooked in this sauce for about an hour on a low heat and served with puréed potatoes or white rice.

Swordfish

Swordfish (*espadarte*) comes particularly from the Sesimbra area south of Lisbon where there is a special swordfish restaurant.

Trout (*truta*) are found inland in northern rivers.

Tuna (*atum*) is caught in May and June off Vila Real and Tavira in the Algarve. Fresh tuna is excellent fried like steak in thin, firm slices. It can be served cold in an hors d'oeuvre salad with an *escabeche* sauce of onion, olive oil, garlic and white wine vinegar.

Whiting (*pescadinha*) can also be served cold.

5

SHOPPING
FOR
GROCERIES

Portugal has been a little slower perhaps than other European countries in adopting hypermarkets and the all-in-one, supermarket style of shopping. It is still very much a place where the little corner or neighbourhood shop flourishes as well as daily fish, vegetable and flower markets. But supermarkets do exist all over the country, though the biggest chains are mainly found in the main cities. Names to look for are Pao de Acucar ('sugar bread') and Mondelo, as well as the more familiar Spar stores. There is a large Pao de Acucar near Cascais on the sea road. Smaller towns and communities have their mini-markets, which are self-service and perhaps easier for the self-caterer to cope with, though it is a good plan to make a shopping list in English and Portuguese using words from the glossary section in this book and take it with you when you shop. It is surprising how alike paper bags of salt and sugar look when you do not know the language.

In general, the larger food shops are open from 9.30am. Some may shut for lunch, reopening around 3 or 4pm until 7.30pm. But times vary with the season and region. Supermarkets are often open till about 10pm.

Probably less easy to use for the tourist with little Portuguese are the small, family-run stores known as *lugas*. An excellent example is that belonging to Lurdes and her husband near the Ritz Hotel and prison in Lisbon (like their surroundings *lugas* are highly democratic and cater to all levels of society). Here Julia, an old hen, lives and clucks behind the counter; a caged canary sings by the door hanging among the smoked hams; and an immense tortoiseshell cat lazes on a cushion on the counter. Lurdes goes to the main Praca de Ribeiro market each day to bring back a selection of best buys in fresh vegetables and fruit. The shop otherwise mainly stocks wines, meat and dry goods. The name *luga* means 'a place', and these shops become little cer.tres of gossip as well as sources of merchandise. The ceilings support as much produce as the shelves; strings of garlic hang along with bunches of the fresh, pungent coriander essential to many Portuguese dishes.

Small specialist shops include *charcutaria*, where pork products, delicatessen and sausage items, smoked hams, meats and cheeses are sold; fresh bread is also often sold here. The *pasteleria* is the place for those famous local sweetmeats. Drinks, tea and coffee are often also available, making the *pasteleria* a rendezvous for shoppers. The *pasteleria* is of Moorish origin and later came to sell cakes made by the nuns at local convents. Breads, pastries and sweetmeats are the main buys here but there are also savoury butters to serve with snacks before a meal or to spread on toast. *Mercearia* is the name for a grocer. *Farmacia* is the pharmacy/drug store where, in addition to medicinal items, one buys baby foods (see below).

Lisbon lacks high-class speciality food shops like Fauchon in Paris, but this may change with the opening of Michel Costa's *O Grand Circo da Comeda*. This, the chef says, will look like a circus with a glass roof, the space cooled by a waterfall. Magicians and jugglers will entertain people at the complex of restaurants and food shops in the 750 square metre building. Charcuterie, patisserie, chocolates and pasta will be on sale. There will be take-out foods as well as 250-seat restaurants with circus shows and classical music at night. At 87 Avenida Marques de Tomar, the restaurants will offer fixed-price menus for less than 1000 *escudos* per person.

Lisbon does have several fine supermarket-style food shops that are well worth a visit. The nearest equivalent to Zabar's, Fortnum and Mason or Harrods' food hall is Martins e Costa, 39 Rua do Carmo, which sells quality foods and delicatessen produce. Jeronimo Martins in Rua Garrett is another similar shop selling a wide variety of groceries, including many imported items, as well as wines. Celeiro (81 Rue 1 de Dezembro and other locations in Lisbon) is used by many foreigners resident in the city for its good selection of imported goods, such as English teas and biscuits, as well as its excellent fresh fish, meat, cheeses and wines. The shop also has a diet food section. Though none of these stores is very large, they are neatly and cleanly laid out.

To help the self-caterer in a Portuguese food shop of whatever size, I am listing some common brands of major grocery items. Price indications are based on 1985 prices (when £1 = 200 *escudos* and $1 = 170 *escudos* approximately).

DRY GOODS

Black beans are sold mainly for Brazilian-style dishes using dried meat. Dried beans and peas and chick peas — (*grao*) are sold in markets and *feijao branco* are haricot beans. *Feijao manteiga* are butter beans and white and brown beans are available canned in the Guloso brand at around 126 *escudos* a can.

Kellogg's cereal products are available in larger stores in Portugal and Kellogg's Special costs 500 *escudos* a pack. Cornflakes are 410 *escudos* but if bought in large plastic bags become cheaper at 300 *escudos* for 500 grams. Weetabix costs 365 *escudos* for a box of 24. British imported Farmhouse bran costs about 380 *escudos*.

Rice is available everywhere and the best type to look for is *anulha* ('needle') rice. If you do buy some not too good rice, a Portuguese tip is to fry it before boiling it and this will ensure that the rice grains separate well. Carolino rice at 107 *escudos* is a good quality brand.

DAIRY PRODUCE

Although olive oil is much used for cooking in Portugal the refined olive oil has a unique salty tang — white pork fat called *banha* is on sale in jars and plastic packs in many grocery stores. It is particularly favoured in the north for cooking. It is somewhat akin to our lard and can be substituted for this. *Banha pura de porco* is available in tins and in a pack costs 207 *escudos*. In the North, margarine may be mixed with pig fat. Butter in Portugal is good, salty and golden and costs about 154 *escudos* for a half pound pack. Alpina margarine is around 143 *escudos* for 500 grams; it can be bought with or without salt or half salted. Flora is 158 *escudos* for 500 grams and the Dutch Girassol brand is 457 *escudos* for 500 grams.

Until fairly recently, there was not a wealth of dairy produce in Portugal but the variety and availability are growing. A few years ago, yoghurt was rare. Now it is seen in most supermarkets. Younger mothers have adopted it to feed their children, but only a small number of adults eat it regularly. A brand to look out for is Yoplait at 27 *escudos* a tub for fruit flavours. Ucal natural yoghurt costs about 20 to 26 *escudos* and is sold in little packs complete with a spoon. Eggs are about 80 *escudos* for half dozen of No. 2 size.

Nor has Portugal a great number of cheeses. Twelve years ago very little cheese was eaten. In the centre, east and Spanish border areas it was eaten with a spoon and dried to keep in summer. Now cheese is produced all over the country. The quality has improved, although cheese is often still regarded as a luxury item. The *Serra* cheese in season is extremely expensive and can cost 1625 *escudos* a kilo.

Usually cheese is served in small pieces as an appetiser before a meal and later at the end of the meal. It is rarely used in cooking though there is a Portuguese-made Dutch cheese imitation called *Flamengo* which could be used in cookery. Often cheese is served with cubes or slices of sweet quince preserve which is thick and dry in texture. The quince preserve called *marmelada* is available in groceries, goes well with drinks at the end of a meal, especially with a glass of port.

The *Serra da Estrela* cheese is probably the best known and most sought after. Its main production season is December to July but it is considered at its best from January to April when it is nicely soft and gooey in the middle. Towards July it tends to become harder and drier. It is a salty cheese, slightly sharp in flavour, contained in a rind. It is produced from sheep's milk in the hilly area around the wine town of Viseu in the north.

Serra is a cheese made from the milk of sheep in the Alentejo area. It is drier than *Serra da Estrela* and has a nuttier taste. It is made from February to June and matured for up to two years in cool cellars.

Alcobaca comes from the place where the great monastery is situated and has some of the biggest kitchens for monastic entertaining. It is similar to *Tomar* cheese but larger in rounds, dry and white inside its skin. It should be eaten fresh and kept covered with olive or vegetable oil.

Rabacal is a small goat's milk cheese and *Azeitao*, named for its place of origin just south of Lisbon, is semi-soft, creamy in texture and sharp in taste. Cheeses also come in from the Azores islands made with cow's milk with a firm curd. These are known as *Ilhas* and *Sao Jorge*. These are mature cheeses with a full flavour and a sharp taste and can be used for grating and cooking. The cheese from Pico island in the Azores is spicier in taste.

Many consider *Castelo Branco* cheese to be the best in Portugal. It is made from goat's milk and is hard enough for grating or slicing. Worth searching for is *Queijo Fresco* —

fresh cheese made daily from sheep's milk and often sold in little straw containers. *Queijo Fresco* comes in the form of small flat cylinders and, with its delicate, fresh flavour, is often served as an appetiser sprinkled with salt and pepper with crisp toast and white wine. *Queijo de Manha* (morning cheese), made from cow's or goat's milk, can also be served this way (or, like the French Petit Suisse, with raspberries and strawberries). This cheese costs about 63 *escudos* sold in little boxes.

Requeijao is a farm-made white cheese, firmer and drier than *Queijo Fresco*, scored on top and sold in little straw baskets. It is often served as a dessert with cinnamon and sugar. Alverca cheeses, known as *Queijos Saloios*, are made with a mixture of sheep and goat's milk. These cheeses are small and sometimes have a spicy taste. These too can be served as an hors d'oeuvre.

DIET FOODS

In the bigger supermarkets there are sections devoted to items needed for various diets. In such health food sections one may find anything from Rose's lime juice to cod liver oil and vitamin tablets. Integral is the name of a brand of rice which is considered good for dieters and those who need easily digested foods. Becel is a margarine spread which contains no salt; it costs 100 *escudos*. Caitamo is a brand of sunflower oil for vegetarian cookery, said to be good for those with heart disease or high blood-pressure.

BABY FOODS

Racks of baby foods can be found in pharmacies (*farmacia*). Bledine, costing about 63 *escudos* a jar, is made in formulae to suit babies from 3 months. Nutribem at 70 *escudos* a jar provides a selection of different types of foods — meat, fish, vegetables and fruit; a meat or fish is combined with a vegetable.

BEVERAGES

Nestlés instant milk powder is sold in tins costing about 260 *escudos* for 400 grams. Carnation evaporated milk is 135 *escudos*. Cadbury's hot drink products are available, as well as brands like Milo, Nesquik, Bovril, Ovaltine and Ovalmaltine — all found in larger fine food stores like Jeronimo Martins, which also stock Twinings teas at about 500 *escudos* for a packet of Earl Grey. Tetley's tea bags cost about 122 *escudos* for 25 bags. Lipton and Ridgway are also imported. There is Matte tea from Brazil and the French brand of Pompadour camomile tea is excellent as a soothing late-night drink. Droste chocolate powder is imported from Holland and there is a brand of powder (Tang) with which to make an orange juice drink.

With top grades costing 1300 *escudos* a kilo, coffee is excellent. It is imported from former Portuguese colonies such as Angola, Mozambique and in particular Brazil. Sical is a Portuguese brand-name of good coffee sold in bean or ground form. Nescafé is the main brand of instant coffee as well as Braza, which costs 87 *escudos* for 100 grams.

Mineral waters are sold in plastic bottles of various sizes. Schweppes and Canada Dry products are available in Portugal and Compale is the name of natural fruit juices sold in cans. For hot savoury drinks, Knorr cubes and packet soups are sold.

BISCUITS, BREADS AND PRESERVES

Jacob's biscuits, Danish butter cookies, Hovis crackers and Ryvita can all be found in better Portuguese food shops. Pala Pala is the local brand-name of potato crisps. *Broa* (bread) costs about 61 *escudos* a loaf and an oval wholemeal loaf is around 38 *escudos*. *Pao refueija* is a big round loaf. The Algarve *pao integral* is the sort served with sardines — a round, brown wholemeal loaf made with unrefined flour. *Papa seco* are small white rolls rather like bridge rolls. Italian-made pastas called *Panzani* are imported by Martins e Costa and pastas are sold in most stores. Chinese noodles are also available.

Marmelada, the Portuguese quince preserve, keeps well and honey is a good buy. There is a good brand of jams called Casalba which costs about 119 *escudos* a jar.

COOKING OILS AND FLAVOURINGS

Portugal still clings fairly traditionally to cooking with olive oil and it costs about 214 *escudos* a litre; a good quality oil costs 350-450 *escudos* compared to vegetable oil at 200-218 *escudos* a litre. Andorinha at 370 *escudos* a litre is pure Portuguese olive oil. It is wise to spend a little more to get a good quality oil, especially near the coast, where unbranded oil may have a rank and fishy tang.

Vinegar is cheap at 26 *escudos* for three-quarters of a litre compared with 267 *escudos* for French tarragon vinegar. White wine vinegar can be used instead of wine in many Portuguese recipes and for marinating meat and fish. Sharwoods' range of imported Indian chutneys and curry flavourings are available in the fine food stores and McCormick spices can also be found, though there are good local brands.

Some people get withdrawal symptoms without Heinz tomato ketchup and this is available at around 134 *escudos* for a small bottle compared with Portuguese tomato pulp in a bottle for 86 *escudos*. Guluso brand tomatoes cost about 100 *escudos* for a large can. Hellmann's imported mayonnaise is on sale but local Guluso mayonnaise is 950 *escudos* for a massive 1930cc pot. Mustard is 613 *escudos* for a 2050 gram jar and, again, imported brands like Colmans can be found. Salt is produced mainly aound Aveiro and the Algarve. It costs around 17 *escudos* for a table container. Olives, of course, are available everywhere, sold in little plastic packs at about 50 *escudos*, or in jars at 90 *escudos*.

Some like it hot and chilli infusions like *piri piri* sauce are sold, especially in the Algarve, in little jars. Worcester sauce is available in better supermarkets and curry powder is sold. Portugal's nationally favoured flavouring is *colorau*, a ground dry spice of peppers. The Portuguese use it as freely as salt and pepper and garlic in their fish stews and in marinating meat. One can substitute paprika for a sweeter flavour or cayenne for a spicier taste.

Of the sweet spices, cinnamon is a national love and used scattered on egg puddings. Another well-liked pudding flavouring, *cidrao* — candied lemon peel — is well worth buying to bring home. Chocolate mousse is probably Portugal's second favourite pudding and a suitable chocolate to buy for this is Belleville; a slab costs about 264 *escudos*. Pantagruel is a cooking chocolate that costs about 296 *escudos* for 100 grams. Sugar comes from Madeira and Sidul is a brand of granulated sugar.

6

WINES AND SPIRITS

Portugal was late in introducing modern, scientific methods into its wine growing. Until recent years, production was mostly by peasant farmers using traditional methods. Portugal is, however, the world's fourth largest wine producer. It has been growing vines since the time of the Emperor Probus in 282AD though the Phoenicians were said to have introduced vines to Portugal. Today more than 100 different types of wine are produced in Portugal and the reds, whites and greens reflect most patriotically the colours of the national flag.

Probably the best known of Portuguese wines both in Britain and the States are the rosés. They account for two-thirds of light wine exports and are produced in Vila Real in the Tras os Montes province and increasingly now in other areas. Mateus rosé had a tremendous vogue after it was 'discovered' and written up by Sacheverell Sitwell in 1951. Its bulbous green bottle was made into many a lamp base and the slightly sweet pink wine (it is much drier in Portugal) became associated with those who wanted to try a wine but didn't know too much about choosing one: it went with more or less everything. Mateus' overpopularity made it rather sneered at, but, well chilled on a hot day, it is still a delightful drink. Other similar Portuguese rosés are: Casaleiro; Fonseca, sold in a terracotta bottle; and Lancers, the competitor to Mateus, popular in the United States.

But it is the green wines (*vinho verdes*) that are Portugal's unique offering, accounting for a fifth of total wine production. Though called green (a reference to youth rather than colour) they can in fact be white, red or rosé. The whites are most commonly exported and drunk by visitors, and, although the percentage of reds produced is greater, these are mostly drunk by the Portuguese themselves. The red *vinho verdes* should be well chilled and drunk with a highly flavoured regional dish such as grilled sardines or a *cozido* stew.

The white (or rather pale yellowish in colour) *vinho verdes* are the perfect summer holiday wine. Portugal's wines are among the cheapest to buy in Europe. The wines are drunk very young from March after the autumn's vintage, when grapes are picked fully ripe and fermented and bottled immediately so that malolactic fermentation takes place inside the bottle. This gives *vinho verdes* their characteristic slightly prickly sparkle. The *vinho verdes* are grown in the northern Minho area. The vineyards are not neatly terraced with vines set in straight lines as in many other countries. They seem to grow haphazardly and naturally and look extremely attractive festooned from trees, curling round pillars, strung out on wires, canopied over the ground or even twined into pergolas. The raising of the wines from the earth means they are less harmed by late frosts. The grapes do not get as much reflected sunlight from the ground, but the land underneath can be used to grow other crops such as maize and the *couve* cabbage.

Vinho verdes are low in alcoholic strength: between 8 and 10 per cent (though *Alvarinho* from the far north is made from the single grape variety and is 12° alcohol) and do not improve with keeping. Some labels to look out for are Gambas, Gatao, Lagosta, Aveleda and Casal Garcia. Well chilled, these wines are wonderful drunk as a light summer aperitif or with fish and seafood, sardines and salads. In June, in the Lisbon festival when fish and sardines are sold from stalls in the streets of Alfama, a glass of *vinho verde* is just the right and traditional accompaniment.

Apart from *vinho verdes*, the main category of Portuguese wines is *vinhos maduras* or mature wines. Portugal was one of the first countries to demarcate quality wine regions in 1908; Algarve, Bairrada, and Douro wines were added to the original list in 1978. Each bottle is numbered and bears the legend '*selo de origin*' over its cork (on *vinho verdes* this is a back label). Among the leading mature wines to look out for are those from the following regions:

Alentejo The wines grown near the Spanish border, stored in earthenware containers and oak casks, are considered the best. *Periquita* is the main red grape used here. Names to look out for are Borba (a strong red), Redondo, Reguengos and Vidigueira, the last bearing a portrait of Vasco da Gama on its label. The wines are deep purply plum, rich and deep with a fruity taste. The whites of this region are mid-straw in colour, full in taste.

Algarve Grapes have been grown in the sandstone soil of the Algarve since the thirteenth century and wines exported from the end of the Middle Ages. There are few vines still planted in this region but there are five wine co-operatives to which growers take their grapes to be made into wine. The best known co-operatives are Lagoa and Portimao. Because of the hot climate, the grapes have a high sugar content and the wine tends to be high in alcohol (13 per cent) and low in acidity. The reds go well with food and the dry whites can be drunk as an aperitif or with shellfish. The area produces dry golden aperitif wines: Alfonso III or Algar Seco (the latter from the Lagoa wine co-operative).

Bairrada This area, south of Oporto, produces fruity red wines which have a lasting taste. The name comes from the Portuguese word (*barro*) for the clay soil in which the vines are grown. On average 80 per cent of this wine is red and the rest white and sparkling. The Bairrada wines are kept 18 months in cask and six months in the bottle before they are sold. The bottles are claret style and the best recent vintages have been 1970, 1973, 1975, 1978 and 1980. The whites go well with fish, pasta and paté and the reds with game, roast meats and strong cheeses.

Bucelas is a demarcated area just north of Lisbon producing a light, dry wine which, although slightly acid, ages well. Bucelas is made of *Arinto* grapes and is full and dry. It was much appreciated by Wellington's officers on their Napoleonic campaign in Portugal and the Duke brought back some as a present for the Prince Regent. It was then a sweet wine, but is now light and dry and goes well with fish, poultry and veal.

Carcavelos is a small area north of the Tagus near Estoril, now with a small vineyard, Quinta do Barao, producing a fortified wine that can be dry or sweet. Carcavelos is a pale yellowish topaz colour with a nutty aroma and almond flavour. It can be drunk as an aperitif or dessert wine. In 1752 it was sent by the King of Portugal as a gift to the Chinese court in Peking.

Colares Here, around Sintra, grapes are grown from vines (planted in sand dunes) which escaped the phylloxera disease. Colares is a small area which, though established for over 700 years, is suffering from the spread of suburbia out from Lisbon. The wines, therefore, are somewhat difficult to find. Wind-breaks have to be made from woven cane to protect the vines from the Atlantic gales and salt spray. The wines are 11-12° alcohol. The reds have a high tannin content which gives them a longer life and they develop a silky, velvet taste. They will last happily in the bottle for up to 30 years. Colares wines are well worth searching for. The reds are soft, dark and rich in colour and go well with game or roast beef and pork.

Dao Probably the best known and loved of Portugal's red wines are grown here, on granite highlands in the north with the town of Viseu as the wine centre. The vines are terraced and trained on wires or staked individually in small plots. The name comes from the river Dao which flows through the region. The Dao wines can be compared with Spain's Rioja or France's Burgundy in style. The Daos, blended from a number of grapes, are matured in cask. The reds (80 per cent of output) have an alcohol content of 11 to 13 per cent with high tannin and glycerine contents. By law they must remain in the cask for at least 18 months, though most are matured for 3 to 5 years. The whites must remain in the cask for six months which deepens their colour. The Daos improve with age and are often described as velvety in texture. The reds go extremely well with poultry, game and cheese dishes. The white Daos, drunk young, go well with hors d'oeuvres, chilled soups and savoury mousses. A reliable label to look for is Grao Vasco (red or white) which, aged three years in cask, is named after a well-known Portuguese painter who lived and worked in Viseu. This incidentally is a town worth visiting not just for its wine but also for its narrow cobbled streets and splendid old buildings clustered around a square at the top of a hill. The original painting for the wine label can be seen in one of the buildings in the hilltop square.

Douro Wines from this region are made from the 60 per cent of grapes remaining after the rest go for port wine production. The vines are grown on extremely steep granite and slate terraced slopes. The wines produced are light and fruity. The whites go well with hors d'oeuvres, salads, chicken and are dry with a full nose. The reds are deep in colour and have a well-balanced taste that goes with liver and kidney dishes, stews and casseroles. From the upper Douro comes Ferreirinha Reservas, Barca Velha, which is excellent — rather like a claret. Vila Real is one of the best known of the Douro producing areas.

Estremadura is the largest quality wine producing area in Portugal, situated north west of Lisbon bordering the Atlantic. The best wines are said to come from around Torres Vedras. The reds are light and fruity and go with rice dishes, pasta, veal and poultry. The whites are pale, light and dry with a fruity taste. They are drunk with salads, poultry and fish.

Lafoes This area in northern Portugal lies between the *vinho verde* and Dao wine regions. The whites from here are pale, light and with a higher than average acidity; they can be drunk as an aperitif. The reds are light, fruity and acidic and go well, lightly chilled, with spicy foods.

Pinhel The northern part of the Dao region produces medium-bodied reds. The whites are medium- to dark-straw in colour and have a full dry taste. They go well with soups and rice dishes and can be drunk as an aperitif.

Ribatejo is the Tagus valley north-east of Lisbon. Here pale but fruity whites and very dark ruby-coloured, fruity reds are produced. The reds are said to have a blackcurrant-like taste when young, developing a roundness with age. Some of the best *garrafeira* wines — reserve wines specially selected by a producer for careful ageing in his own cellars — are made in the Ribatejo. The Ribatejo whites should be drunk with fish, veal and poultry and the reds (at room temperature) with meat and game served with a rich sauce.

Setubal is a sardine canning town south of Lisbon in the Arrabida. Its sweet dessert wine, Moscatel de Setubal, has been compared with the French Beaune de Venise. It is a lovely wine to sip gently with fresh fruit such as peaches or strawberries or after a meal with nuts and biscuits.

Some of the branded wines to note include Serradayres from Ribeiro and Ferreira (Lisbon shippers). These are blended wines, red or white, which are lighter than the Daos but which make excellent table wines. Periquita (from Jose Maria da Fonseca) from the Arrabida area is a good red wine — mature and with plenty of body. Fonseca, whose lovely headquarters at Azeitao can be visited, also sell 100-year-old Moscatel Velho de Torno Viagem which has been matured on a round sea voyage to Brazil.

Sparkling wines

In addition to the very slightly sparkling *vinho verdes*, Portugal produces a range of sparkling wines made in the north by the champagne method. These come in various grades of sweet and dry up to *brut*. The best come from the Bairrada near the north coast and Lamego near the port wine area. There are pink *espumantes*, which can seem a little sickly sweet, and, for those who really like their wines dry, Raposeira Brut de Brut is worth asking for. *Seco* (dry) and *meio seco* (medium-dry) are for those who like sparkling wines a little sweeter.

BUYING WINE IN PORTUGAL

There are usually good selections in supermarkets where one can compare prices. Or, look for *adegas* (wine cellars) where wines are sold from the cask; the transaction will be even cheaper if you take along your own empty bottle.

The Englishman's Drink

Port wine (*porto*) is a drink which has done a great deal to cement the friendship between Portugal and Britain. The English first discovered port in the second crusade when ships en route to fight the Unbeliever were forced by storms to shelter in the harbour at Oporto (now Portugal's second city) on the north coast. The Portuguese persuaded the English that their cause could be as well served fighting the Infidel in Portugal as in Africa. Much later, after the Moors had been driven out, the Treaty of Windsor (1386) allowed the English free trade and travel in Portugal. The earliest English traders with Portugal were known as rag merchants since they sent cloth and cotton to Lisbon, bringing back fruits, sugar, salt, wax, cork, honey, spices and wines.

By the Treaty of Methuen in 1703 (during one of Britain's frequent quarrels with France), port was given tax preference over French claret in Britain; at this time port was a red table wine with a *vinho verde* ancestry rather than a fortified wine. Shipping the red wine back to Britain led to the addition of grape brandy to arrest the rapid fermentation arising from grapes rich in sugar.

In Doctor Johnson's time, red wine from Oporto was widely consumed in Britain; often claret was laced with port. The good doctor declared, 'Claret is for boys and port is for men' (though Boswell thought the wine somewhat acidic). The addition of brandy for fortification in the eighteenth century made port a richer, gentler drink to enjoy at the end of a meal.

By the beginning of the nineteenth century, Britain was drinking over 36 million bottles of port a year, and in the 1930s drank half the total amount of port produced. Though consumption declined with the dawn of the cocktail era, we still consume 90 per cent of vintage port. In 1984, 14 million bottles (a rise of $3\frac{1}{2}$ million compared with ten years ago) were drunk in Britain. The ceremonies of passing the port at service and other dinners is religiously observed and vintage ports are carefully laid down years before to age in a cellar or given as a christening present to a child or godchild. The value of port — still known as the 'Englishman's drink' — is greatly prized judging by the record £1250 paid by an American in 1985 for a 1931 bottle.

The luxury and elegance associated with port wine is not evident in the upper reaches of the Douro river where the grapes are grown. This is an area of rough high granite mountains swept with icy winds in winter, stiflingly hot in summer. It is a landscape apparently unyielding to improvement by man: crowbars and explosives had to be used to beat the rocks into terraces for vine growing. The upper area (Cima Corgo) produces a smaller amount of higher-quality wine than the Baixa (lower) Corgo.

In the old days, it was impossible to bring the wine over the haughty mountains for shipment at Oporto and the casks were brought down river on specially designed boats called *rebelos* which had a somewhat hairy passage over the rapids. Now these boats, apart from one or two kept by the port houses for public relations purposes, have given way to rail or road haulage. But still, to earn its name, port must be shipped over the sandbar at the mouth of the river Douro. In Oporto, the port section of the city is across the river to the south, at Vila Nova de Gaia, where appointments to see the lodges where the port is stored can be made through shippers in Britain.

In the making of port, when enough colour has been produced from the grape skins (and, as well as using modern machinery, some grapes are still trodden by foot in stone troughs), the producer mixes the half fermented wine with a quantity of grape brandy. This stops fermentation and leaves the wine at the required level of sweetness (about 110 litres of brandy is added to 440 litres of wine). The alcoholic strength of port is 19–22° for the red, 16.5–20° for the white. Early in the year following the vintage the wine is transported from the Douro in oak casks holding about 115 gallons each to lodges or warehouses in Vila Nova de Gaia.

There are three main categories of port: wood port which is matured in casks and shipped and bottled when it is ready to drink, and vintage port and crusted port, both of which spend only a short time in cask, maturing in the bottle. These categories are further broken down into the following types:

Wood Port

Ruby Port is the youngest of the wood ports and, therefore, fuller-bodied, robust and of a deep, ruby-red colour. This is matured in cask for 3 to 5 years and then bottled. It is for those who like a sweet port. An example available in the UK is Cockburn's Fine Old Ruby port.

Tawny Port is older than ruby port. Aged 10 to 20 years, it is blended from wines coming from different years, which ensures a continuity of style. Kept for a long time in casks, these ports become lighter in shade (tawny or brownish), lighter in body and richer in bouquet. They can be served chilled or with ice and go well with paté and appetisers. Examples are Harvey's Directors Bin, an aged tawny, and Cockburn's ten-year-old tawny.

White Port is made from white grapes and can be dry to medium-sweet. It is particularly good when chilled. In Portugal, and often in France, white port is drunk nationwide as an aperitif and it can also be drunk after a meal. In the UK Sandeman's new branded white port, Apitiv, is designed for mixing; they also have a fine white port.

Crusted Ports

Though usually blended from different vintages of wine, these are of high quality. After several years in the cask, the port is kept in the bottle, where it throws a crust like a vintage port. It must, therefore, be decanted before being drunk. The colour is usually a full, deep red but the port has a delicate, fruity flavour.

Vintage Port

Vintage Port — the great love of the British — arises from an exceptional year when the shipper has set aside a quantity of the best wine for the purpose. It is kept in the cask in Oporto for two years before bottling. The wine is then matured in the bottle for ten years or more, during which time it throws a sediment known as a crust and needs to be carefully decanted. A good vintage port continues to improve in the bottle for several decades. Recent vintage years are: 1947, 1948, 1950, 1954, 1955, 1958, 1960, 1963, 1966, 1967, 1970 and 1975.

Late Bottled Vintage (LBV) is coming into popularity. This is port of a single vintage year matured in cask rather than in the bottle. Red and full-bodied, it must be bottled before reaching five years of age. It has to be approved by the Port Wine Institute as being worthy of its description.

Though in Britain we may be familiar with port names like Sandeman, Cockburn, Taylors and Harveys, there are many more names in Portugal and it is worthwhile exploring the wine sections of the supermarkets in the holiday areas and trying a few less well-known names. Prices in Portugal are extremely reasonable, starting from 350 *escudos* a bottle (compared with whisky which can cost 400 *escudos* a glass).

If you visit Lisbon and really want to know more about the varieties of port, then visit the Solar de Velho Porto (Port Institute Wine Bar) at 45, Rua Sao Pedro de Alcantara, where a couple of hundred different types of port wine are on sale by the bottle or glass at the long bar or at big round tables in a cool, cavernous room. The bar is open from mid-day till midnight.

A couple of drink ideas based on port and suggested by the firm of Sandeman make good holiday drinking. Port Fizz is simply made by topping up a good measure of port in a tumbler with sparkling white lemonade, a slice of lemon and ice. The Bishop is a classic recipe dating from the eighteenth century. Stud a lemon (or bitter orange if available) with cloves and heat for a few minutes in a low oven while a half pint ($^1/_4$ litre) of water, spiced with cinnamon, allspice, ginger, and cloves, is allowed to boil until it is reduced by half. Pour into a separate pan a bottle of Ruby port, bring to the boil, flame briefly to reduce the spirit, and add the spiced water and lemon. Stir well and heat gently for about ten minutes. Rub the zest off a lemon with a lump of two of sugar and mix this in the bottom of the serving jug with the juice of half the lemon, pour into the hot port and serve immediately.

Madeira Wines

The island of Madeira, which gives its name both to the wine and the cake, was discovered by the Portuguese under Henry the Navigator in 1419. Madeira means 'wood' and the island was at that time covered with dense forest, rising rich and thick on its damp volcanic slopes. The fire lit to clear it raged for seven years and the resulting ash benefits the vines even today. On the orders of Henry the Navigator, the Portuguese planted vines, especially the *malvasia* (or malmsey) from Crete. The Madeiran table wines were exported by English and Scottish merchants who settled there in the late seventeenth century.

In the eighteenth century, the wine was fortified and made on the *solera* system, similar to sherry. It was originally fortified to withstand long sea voyages, though it was found the buffeting improved it. The maturing of Madeira wine is unique since, after the first fermentation, the wine is put in hot rooms called *estufas* and heated to between 30° and 60°C for six months and then slowly cooled. Spirit is then added and the wine is matured in wood casks. While still in the cask, it continues to improve for up to a century, although there is heavy evaporation loss with the passage of time. All the Madeira wines have a unique burnt flavour and an alcoholic strength of 17 to 19°. In Lisbon recently, in the private cellar of wine expert Lopo Cancella de Abreu, I was able to sample an 1880 *verdelho* Madeira: it was perfectly smooth and excellent to savour.

There are four main types of Madeira, named after the grapes from which they are made. Malmsey is a dark, rich, full wine — the sweetest and heaviest of the four. It should be served as a dessert wine with sweets, fruits or cheeses and it goes well with coffee. In Madeira they like to serve it with strawberries and cream. In the eighteenth century, Lopo Cancella told me, ladies used sweeter Madeiras as a perfume for their handerchiefs. *Bual* (or *boal*), another rich dessert wine, is sweet and more delicate in flavour than Malmsey. It is often of higher quality and has a good fruity taste. *Verdelho* is lighter in colour and body and drier than Bual. It can be kept to a great age. It has a golden and dry finish and is more of an all-purpose wine. It can be served as an aperitif, and with hors d'oeuvres such as melon and soup, as well as after a meal; or it is often served mid-morning with a slice of cake. *Sercial*, the driest of the four, has a slightly bitter tang reminiscent of nuts. Pale and light, it makes a good aperitif or it can be served with soups.

Visitors to Madeira can sample and buy wines at the Madeira Wine Association's old beamed premises at Avenida Arriaga, 28 in Funchal.

Spirits

Imported spirits are available in Portugal, but they are expensive. Many visitors prefer, therefore, to search out locally made spirits and liqueurs at low prices. Gin is made in Portugal and, unless you are a purist and stick to your duty-frees, it is fine in cocktails and mixed drinks. Pheysey's Silver Top is about 450 *escudos* a bottle. Other gins are Blandy Brothers Tower of London and McCaffery's, both at 537 *escudos* per bottle. Smirnoff bottled in Portugal is about 640 *escudos* a bottle.

Brandy is made in Portugal and good labels include: Constantino Velha, Carvalho Ribeira, Ouro Velho from Fonseca, VSOP, Fim de Seculo, and Caves Velhas. The best brandies can cost up to 1800 escudos a bottle. Reliquia, and the VSOP's Neto Costa and Ramos Pinto are also highly recommended. There is a rough brandy known as *aguardente* which many visitors find too powerful and fiery and a kind of marc known as *bagaceira*, made from the residue of crushed grapes and skins, which costs about 350 *escudos* per bottle.

In the Algarve, there are local liqueurs of Medronho made from arbutus (juniper) berries in the Monchique area. Also from the Algarve is Licor de Amendoa Amarho (liqueur of bitter almonds) and Pisan Ambon, a liqueur used as a mixer in drinks. Ginja is a yellow cherry liqueur and Ginjinha a sweet cherry liqueur costing about 774 *escudos* a bottle. From the Azores island of Pico comes a *verdelho*-like drink called Pico which was once served to the Czars.

Soft Drinks

Fanta is the national brand of canned fruit drinks and Schweppes products are also available, bottled, in Portugal. Coke is widely sold and Sumol is a local orange drink. Glacear is the brand-name of a club soda. Tap water is usually safe to drink, but mineral waters are widely available. In Portugal, the phrase 'poor man's champagne' refers to a glass of wine to which sparkling mineral water has been added — a good choice for drivers and dieters on a hot day. The most common sparkling bottled waters are: Carvalhelhos, Vimeira, Melgaco, Pedras Salgadas. Non-sparkling brands include: Luso, Agua de Bela Vista (in the Setubal area) and Monchique (Algarve).

7
WHAT TO TAKE WITH YOU

The plus of a self-catering holiday is the freedom to eat what you like when you like. It need not be a chore. Make use of local produce and arrange an easy system of meals. A light breakfast in Portugal can be simply rolls, fresh from the local baker, coffee, fruit juice and preserves. Lunch can be a picnic on the beach, in the mountains, or one of my favourite spots, perched on a cliff at Cape St Vincent, the south-west corner of Europe and the most westerly part of the Algarve. I eat snuggled into a cleft in the rocks and watching shipping plunging into European waters from the Atlantic; an exhilarating experience. Or, if you rent a villa with a pool, a barbecue or salad lunch is marvellous round the water.

In the evening, it is inexpensive to eat out occasionally (see chapter 12) but also relaxing to prepare a meal in your apartment or villa. Planning is essential so you have all the ingredients you need and do not end up with piles of wasted food. I think the two most important things to take with you on a self-catering holiday anywhere are a notebook and a menu glossary (see chapter 13). You can then make up shopping lists in advance, even on the plane going over, and not have to worry during the holiday.

The first days are the worst, dealing with unfamiliar equipment and surroundings, language and lack of knowledge as to where the best local shops are found. The better villa-renters leave information on shops and shopping hours in the villas and some provide a 'welcome pack' of basics so at least you have the makings of a meal when you arrive tired after the journey. It may be at a weekend or festival (see page 20) when everything is shut. To cover such emergencies, it is wise to take along some foods such as packet soups, some pasta and tinned meat, which will not get wasted over the holiday. A jar of powdered milk and some butter are also useful. Butter, though more available in Portugal (and nicely salty) than in some Mediterranean countries, is expensive and it's best to use vegetable or olive oil for cooking. Packet soups can be used as instant sauces, gravies and bases for casseroles as well as soups and do not take much room in the luggage.

As a self-catering unit gives you space to launder and there is not the need to show off with different clothes for every meal as in some hotels, luggage space for clothes can be reduced and used for a few kitchen comforts. The more travel-happy can be packed in the main case well wrapped in plastic bags (lots of plastic bags are invaluable for picnics and storing food). I'd add in a roll of cling-film and kitchen foil. There are never enough storage containers for food and something is needed to wrap foods for happier, mess-free picnics.

More perishable foods can be packed in one of the Thermos Keep it Cool bags in white or denim blue with capacities of 16 and 22 litres. These insulated bags are square with zip tops and sturdy carrying handles which can pack flat or be used as hand-luggage and later beach and picnic bags. They can be wiped clean and sachet ice packs can be taken along, frozen in the ice box of the fridge and popped in to keep foods cool for picnics. Also useful is a Thermos flask for hot and cold drinks and food flasks with wide necks in which baby foods can also be carried. Thermos also make large Keep it Cool jugs with drip-proof dispenser — fine for taking lots of soft drinks to the beach or having round the pool to eliminate frequent trips indoors for refills. This may be rather bulky if travelling other than by car. A newer idea from the same company is a soft insulated bag for carrying wine bottles. Chilled *vinho verde* for picnics needs to be kept well chilled for the best enjoyment. If you do not have a cooler bag or Thermos, wrap the cold bottles in newspaper soaked in cold water and place in a secure, thick plastic bag to carry.

Although shops in Portugal's tourist areas are well aware of English tastes and foods, it might be as well to take a few foods that the family like, such as shrink-wrap packs of bacon, favourite tea blends, coffee (although excellent in Portugal, it can be cheaper here). Portugal is not too rich in cheese, but vacuum packs of favourite types from home travel well and can also be used in cooking. Portugal has good preserves but Gold and other low-fat diet aids in their own plastic packs should be sealed in plastic bags and sent in hold luggage where it is usually colder.

Among the dried goods, it is worth taking a small bag of flour if you are not going to need more than a spoonful or two to thicken sauces or coat a piece of meat or fish, and buying a big bag could be a waste. If you are staying in a place remote from shops, a few packs of McDougall's yeast bread mixes ready to blend and bake are useful standbys and can also be used to make simple pizza bases.

Although rented accommodation is usually fully equipped and renters will provide lists of what is included, I always like to take a favourite sharp kitchen knife (pack it in hold luggage or you'll run the risk of having it removed in airport security checks), a tin-opener, corkscrew (just in case), apron, oven-gloves to shield one from unexpectedly hot pan handles and oven doors, and, if you are a fanatical tea-drinker, a teapot. Portugal — used to the English over the years and where many local women drink tea in preference to coffee — is more likely to have teapots and kettles in its rented accommodation than other European countries.

Portuguese kitchens, particularly many in the Algarve (where many of the older villas were designed and built by British owners) are extremely attractive with tiled walls and often marble worktops. Cookers will be electric (220 volts) or fuelled by Calor gas. Ovens everywhere can be very temperamental and vary in temperature, but since the Portuguese tend to cook their dishes on top of the stove, most of the recipes in this book have been geared to this and the few oven casserole ideas will not be too dependent on exact temperature and timing. Most villas and apartments will have some maid service and maids will help explain equipment and any problems even by sign language. Again, they are used to the British. There are also cook services run by English women in the Algarve for those who want to splash out and give a special dinner party without worrying about shopping and cooking.

Other extras to take along include a supply of matches (enough are rarely provided and could be damp) and some candles, not just in case the power fails, but because it is rather romantic to dine by candlelight. Souvenir shops sell the elaborately carved and decorated candles from the north of the country which would be fine for a special dinner, but extravagant for incidental lighting.

Those plastic bags which carried down extra foods, herbs and favourite seasonings are invaluable to wrap and store foods and with holes in them can be used as a salad drainer. Thicker bags with the corner clipped away can be used as piping bags if you are going to be that decorative about holiday food. A wine bottle or milk bottle acts as a substitute rolling pin.

Portugal is happily one of those countries where if there is not quite enough equipment in the kitchen for your needs, it is easy and cheap to buy something locally and perhaps take it home as a souvenir. Thin battered metal pots and pans are often the staple cooking utensils in self-catering establishments and in Portugal the use of earthenware is something which thankfully has not died out and these pots and plates make cheap, if cumbersome and fragile souvenirs to take and use at home. In markets as at Loule, Portimao and other Algarvean places as well as in markets and household shops all over the country, earthenware dishes and platters of all sizes and shapes can be bought cheaply and can be used on top of the stove directly on the heat. The individual round dishes with little handles, the *frigideiras* (about 100 *escudos* each) used to cook steaks, cut washing up by going straight from stove to table and look charming. Larger casserole pots and big dishes for rice or meats are available. In the north at Barcelas is one of Portugal's best markets for buying earthenware where it comes in deep brown, decorated with yellow flecked bird and flower designs. Fan-shaped dishes are traditionally used to serve rice with meats and there are oval, flat serving dishes decorated with fish. A fun buy is a ribbed earthenware dish, often in the shape of a pig on which small sausages can be barbecued in flamed brandy as an aperitif snack.

In Lagoa, this cheap basic pottery used to be found drying outside the potter's house but is rarer now. Pottery using Moorish bird and flower motifs has been revived at Porches and buys here will make lovely fruit dishes and wall decorations.

Some of the bigger earthenware dishes have wickerwork baskets in which to serve them on the table and in the Algarve baskets for bread and fruit are made in esparto grass; baskets are also available in raffia and cane. Wickerwork items are imported from Madeira. In Lisbon there are two well-known companies making ceramics — well worth a visit to see Portuguese traditional designs.

The first, founded in 1849 is Viuva Lamego, Largo do Intendente 25, which produces thick plates in cottagey designs, often blue and red on white with heart motifs, as well as wall fountains, tiles and huge soup tureens. Vista Alegre, founded in 1824, at 18 Largo do Chiado, is Portugal's best-known company for fine porcelain. They will decorate plates to order and sell reproductions of India Company china designs. Atlantis is the name of Portugal's full lead crystal company which has outlets in Portimao and Lagos in the Algarve.

Buying kitchen and cooking equipment in Lisbon, the Rua da Vitoria is the place with household utensil shops interspersed with small restaurants. Here Solmar, at number 69, sells everything for the kitchen. There are still many small shops to be found around the country where metal cook pots are made up to order and one will see lots of *chinos* hanging up. This is a conical shaped utensil with holes in the sides, but the bottom solid. Many Portuguese housewives still puree and blend ingredients in these *chinos*, forcing food through with the help of a wooden pestle (rather too elbow grease consuming for those used to a Magimix). Large, heavy enamelled pans, a deep earthenware pot for making chicken dishes such as *frango na pucara* and big heart-shaped dishes for rice are other Portuguese cooking and serving containers.

In Lisbon, at 34 Travessa Nova de S. Domingos and 4 Rua Autao Vaz de Almada, and in Oporto, at 124-134 Rua Alexandre Braga, is Braz e Braz, a multi-storey source of everything for the kitchen and home. It is the place to buy all kinds of Portuguese ceramics from the basic country earthenware to the cabbage leaf nineteenth-century copies from Coimbra. There are also blue and white copies of seventeenth-century Coimbraga pottery (a little round dish will cost about 200 *escudos*); eighteenth-century reproductions, Chinese imports from Macau, and terrines made in the shape of ducks. One can buy moulds here in which to make the *pudim* flan from about 110 *escudos*; aluminium boxes for carrying hot food to the office for lunch which could be used for picnics; big copper pans for 2000 *escudos*; and brass scales for 2240 *escudos* (old-fashioned scales feature much as a decorative item in Portuguese homes).

A tip from the sales lady at Braz e Braz is to soak the earthenware *frigideira* and other earthenware platters (costing from only 64 *escudos* a piece) and items which are going directly on the heat in cold water for 24 hours before the first use. A big casserole dish in earthenware is about 200 *escudos*.

At Braz e Braz one can buy the Algarvean *cataplana*. This is believed to date from Moorish times and consists of two metal saucer-shaped lids which interlock firmly together. The Algarvenas will cook almost anything in it from fish to game but their most famous dish is the one which combines pork, clams, herbs, onions in white wine and seasonings. The *cataplana* can be shaken and turned over during cooking without opening so food is more evenly cooked and the device acts as a primitive pressure-cooker, keeping in all the steam. The *cataplana* is customarily brought to table unsealed and opened in front of the diners so that they get the full effect of the scent of released food steam. Without a *cataplana*, similar recipes can be cooked in a saucepan with a very tightly fitting lid.

A new piece of equipment, inspired by the *cataplana* and invented by Michel Costa, Lisbon's nouvelle cuisine chef is what he calls the 'catavap', which has recently gone on sale. Though the *cataplana* is perhaps found more in restaurants than private homes, the catavap is useful in creating a lighter, healthier meal. It can be used for steaming on a shelf inside a good-looking wok-shaped base with fitting domed lid around which the heat runs, therefore making cooking times faster as the steam moves round the food more economically and uses less fuel. There are brass handles on the aluminium body which make it look attractive enough to bring to the table. Later the catavap will be made in copper and stainless steel. In Portugal it costs about 13-1400 *escudos*. The catavap, says Michel Costa, can be used as a steamer, to make stews, as a wok, to cook chicken and fish; and the traditional *cataplana* dishes will work well, too. Michel says it is easier to manage than a *cataplana* and is not too heavy to handle.

Another almost essential piece of equipment for Algarvean cooking is the *fogareiro*, which is available in most parts of Portugal but in the south's hotter climate is an aid for eating out round the pool, on the beach for impromptu barbecues or even if the oven won't function. It is small (about a foot in height) and made from cast iron — a barbecue standing on its own plinth. Too heavy for ease of bringing home — (though I did bring one back and the airline managed to crack it in transit), it can be moved around to where it is needed and used to grill Portuguese sausages, sardines and meats as required. Many apartment complexes and villas will have some kind of permanent barbecue built into the garden or patio and, to aid meals here, particularly when serving fish, invest in wire food holders available in ironmongers round the country. With handles and two sides to hold the food safely, they can be turned to cook food evenly without it breaking or falling into the fire.

It is worth going to the market at Loule, up the almond-shaded lanes leading inland, to buy fruit and vegetables and also some of the copper pans and other utensils made here which look splendid polished up in any kitchen.

Easy to carry souvenirs of table linen are good buys in Portugal where much hand embroidery is still done. In the Algarve there are esparto grass mats to buy, and from the north come thick linen mats and tablecloths embroidered often blue on white or beige on white with traditional hearts and crosses motifs. Madeira is well known for its exquisite embroidery work — an industry as important as wine and tourism in earnings that was originally organised into a business by an English lady, Miss Phelps, who lies buried in Funchal's Protestant cemetery. The work is imported for the mainland souvenir shops and table linen, aprons, handkerchiefs and other items are available.

Portugal is the world's leading grower of cork and items made from this make good light presents to bring home. In Lisbon Mr Cork (alias A. Gama Reis) at 4-10 Rua da Escola Politecnica has the most amazing array of items made from cork. If he likes you, the proprietor will offer a glass of his personal port and talk about his famous customers. You can buy thin sheets of cork for letter writing, handbags, buckets (*tarros*) from the Alentejo, a floating bar set for the swimming pool or just a floating ashtray for those who smoke in the bath.

8

MEALS FOR TWO

Sharing a holiday for two in a small apartment means the need for simpler, appetising and flavoursome dishes that do not take much time to prepare and yet give a good taste of Portugal and make economical use of products that are easily available.

The *cataplana*, if available, can be used as a simple pressure-cooker and is available in small sizes for domestic use. Or a pan with a tight-fitting lid can be used, shaking it occasionally during cooking. It means tender meats and fish without the need to struggle with an erratic oven. The steaming process will tenderise tough meats and bring out flavours.

You can experiment with what is available to create your own *cataplana* recipes but here are some basic mixes that are typically Portuguese.

Partridge with walnuts
Brown the partridge in margarine or butter. Add chopped parsley to taste, chopped onion and a bay leaf. Place in *cataplana* and add 2 liqueur glasses of brandy, 50 grams/2oz ground walnuts for each partridge and ¼ litre/½ pint good white wine. Cook in the closed *cataplana* for 20 minutes.

Stewed chicken
Place a prepared chicken in a *cataplana* with plenty of chopped tomatoes and onions, 1 clove garlic, sherry glass full of port wine and season to taste. Cook for 30 minutes.

Partridge with cockles or clams
Fry the partridge in butter or margarine with chopped garlic and a bay leaf. Place in *cataplana* and add port wine and some cockles or clams. Cook for 25 minutes; add chillies if wished to taste.

Roast meat with almonds

Brown meat all over in a pan with margarine, oil, or lard and with chopped onions. Place in *cataplana* with a little butter and a sherry glass full of port. Simmer gently. Add ground almonds and a little water and close the *cataplana*. Cook for 20 minutes if meat is tender — more if tough — adding more wine as necessary.

Tomato and orange soup

(Sopa de tomates e laranja)

A cool and creamy throat-soother for starting a meal or with a salad at lunchtime. This soup can be served hot or cold and makes use of Portugal's abundant tomato supplies.

450g/1lb tomatoes	1 bay leaf
1 onion	575ml/1 pint light stock
1 carrot	6g/¼oz flour
1 strip of lemon rind	salt, pepper
18g/³⁄₄ oz butter	rind and juice of ½ an
75ml/¹⁄₈ pint single cream	orange

Chop the tomatoes, slice the onions and carrot and put in a pan with lemon rind, bay leaf, stock and salt and pepper. Cover and simmer till the tomatoes are pulpy — about 30 minutes — then liquidise or blend. In a separate pan, melt butter, add flour, and pour on liquid. Blend and bring to the boil. Add juice from a small orange and shredded and blanched orange rind. Season and stir in cream.

Minho eggs

(Ovos a minhota)

A quick snack dish for anytime of day or evening or as a dinner starter.

1 sliced onion	2 eggs
1 large skinned tomato	chopped basil (optional)
oil or butter for cooking	
seasoning	

Cook onion and roughly chopped tomato together in a pan till tender. Season to taste. Add a sprinkling of herbs such as basil if wished. Meanwhile butter two small tins or cocotte dishes and break an egg into each. Bake in the oven till the whites are set and remove from dishes. Serve on top of the onion and tomato mixture.

Shrimps with cream and port
(Camaroes con creme e vinho do Porto)

This is an idea from the house of Sandeman to enrich shrimps. Chop shelled shrimps finely, add chopped onions fried in butter. Pour a little port over the mixture in the pan and simmer for a few minutes. Add about 15 ml/1 table-spoon of cream and 1 egg-yolk per person and salt and pepper to taste. Spoon into small, ovenproof dishes and reheat in the oven till set.

Frying steaks or fish in the little *frigideira* earthenware dishes common in Portugal saves washing up as the dishes go from stove top to table keeping the contents extra hot. Slow cooking of steak in this way with onions helps make the meat more tender.

Steak on a platter
(Bife a frigideira)

2 steaks	*1 bay leaf*
butter or oil for cooking	*2 thick slices ham*
2 garlic cloves	*2 slices bread*
15ml/1 tablespoon white wine (or wine vinegar)	*salt and pepper*

Fry the steak slowly to medium rare in a frying pan (or prefer-ably the individual earthenware dishes), with chopped garlic, wine and bay leaf. Put steaks on one side and remove bay leaf. Fry a thick slice of ham and a slice of bread in the sauce. Season to taste. Serve in the cooking dish with the steak on top of the bread and the ham on top of the steak. For *Bife Chave Douro*, a fried egg can be substituted for the ham. Lemon juice can be sprinkled over the meat for flavour as they do in Portugal.

Algarve tuna steak
(Bife de Atum a Algarvia)

A similar treatment but with tuna steaks this time. Tinned

tuna can be used but the fresh steaks of the fish are available in May and June in the Algarve and then slices should be cooked as the fish is very filling and needs some kind of sauce to prevent it seeming too dry.

2 onions
350g/12oz tinned or fresh
  tuna

125g/4oz fat bacon
1 glass white wine

Fry the sliced onion with the bacon. When the onion is soft and the bacon almost cooked, add the tuna and wine and heat through gently for about 10 minutes, stirring occasionally but taking care not to break the fish up. Serve with vegetables or salad.

You may find frozen trout in supermarkets coming from the rivers of northern Portugal. This recipe marinates them before grilling.

Grilled trout with orange

(Truta grelhados com laranja)

Marinade:
30ml/2 tablespoons white
  wine vinegar
grated rind or juice of ½ an
  orange
1 small onion finely chopped
5 whole black peppercorns

2 sprigs thyme
2 sprigs parsley
salt

2 cleaned trout
grilled orange slice to serve

Mix together ingredients for the marinade. Place trout in a shallow dish, pour the marinade over and cover. Leave in the fridge for 8 hours. Lift trout from the marinade and grill for 5-6 minutes on each side. Serve with grilled orange slices.

Hake is a delightful, under-rated fish found in Portugal. Baked with potatoes and mayonnaise it becomes an easy suppertime dish.

Maia hake

(Pescada a Maiata from the Minho area)

225g/8oz hake fillets (about
  1cm/½ inch thick)

lemon juice
salt

68

225g/8oz potatoes   *1 chopped onion (optional)*
150ml/¼ pint mayonnaise

Trim the fish fillets and put in an oven-proof dish sprinkled with lemon juice and salt. Boil the potatoes, dice and fry lightly in a little olive oil. Add to the fish. Chopped onion can be added on top of the potatoes. Cover the fish and potatoes with mayonnaise, working it into the fish and potatoes. Spread a layer of mayonnaise on top with the back of a spoon. Bake for about half an hour in a medium oven (180C/350F/Gas mark 4) till it rises like a soufflé on top. A little olive oil can be added if necessary during baking.

Another idea for using summery mayonnaise is as a sauce for cooking fish. This is from the Lisbon area.

Wrapped fish delights
(Delicias de peixe envoltas)

2 fish fillets (hake or bass are best); enough for 1 portion each
milk for poaching
breadcrumbs for coating

butter for frying
2 large thin slices of ham
mayonnaise
grated cheese

Poach the fish in the milk, drain and coat lightly with breadcrumbs. Fry in butter. Wrap the fish in the slices of ham which have previously been poached in the milk. Cover with mayonnaise and sprinkle with grated cheese. Brown under the grill or in the oven. Serve with rice or boiled potatoes.

Crab with tawny port
(Caranguejo com vinho do porto)

1 kg/2 lbs crab
87g/3½oz butter
1 glass tawny port
juice of 1 lemon
1 onion
few sprigs parsley

15 ml/1 tablespoon grated cheese
15 ml/1 tablespoon breadcrumbs
salt, pepper

Wash the crab thoroughly and boil whole in water flavoured with the chopped onion, parsley, pepper and salt. Allow crab to cool and open carefully. Throw away the 'dead man's fingers', remove legs and all meat as cleanly as possible. Cut crab meat in small pieces and simmer in a pan for about 30 minutes with butter, lemon juice, port and salt and pepper to taste. Fill the empty, cleaned shell with crab, dust outside with grated cheese and breadcrumbs and place in a medium oven till golden brown.

Though beef and lamb may be rarer finds in Portugal, pork, liver and game are more available and can be used in the following recipes.

Braga cutlets
(Costeletas a moda de Braga)

4-6 pork cutlets (depending
    on size)
350g/12oz potatoes
43g/1³⁄₄oz butter
1¹⁄₂ soup spoons white wine

1 large onion
43g/³⁄₄oz cooking fat
63g/2¹⁄₂oz ham
salt, pepper

Trim cutlets and season with salt and pepper. Sprinkle with a little of the wine and fry in the butter and cooking fat. In a separate pan, lightly fry the potatoes cut in thin slices. Remove cutlets and keep hot. Add chopped ham and onion to the fat in which the cutlets were cooked and fry till golden. Replace the cutlets, with the rest of the wine and potatoes and simmer gently for half an hour, adding more wine if necessary.

Liver is usually marinated and cooked in a *frigideira*. A Lisbon way of cooking liver is to slice it thinly and slice one big onion per portion of liver. Mix a little white wine and a couple of finely chopped garlic cloves in a little bowl with salt and pepper to taste and a bay leaf and leave the liver and onions to marinate in this for an hour or two. Locals will use the pork fat (*banha*) to cook the liver, but butter or lard can equally be used. Melt a little in a pan or earthenware dish and cook the onions till golden and then add the liver and enough of the wine marinade to make a sauce (remove the bay leaf). Season to taste and serve with boiled, sliced potatoes.

A yoghurt finish is also a good way of cooking liver.

Liver in yoghurt

(Iscas com yogurt)

175g/6oz sliced lamb's liver
18g/³/₄oz flour
15ml/1 tablespoon oil
1 large sliced onion
150ml/¹/₄ pint stock
salt, pepper
62ml/2¹/₂ fl oz natural
   yoghurt

2 large skinned, seeded and
   roughly chopped
   tomatoes
15ml/1 tablespoon or less
   piri piri sauce, or
   Worcester sauce

Cut the liver in thin strips, 1cm/¹/₂ inch wide, and toss in seasoned flour. Heat the oil in a large frying pan, add onions and fry gently till soft. Add the liver and cook gently till brown on both sides. Stir in stock and piri piri or Worcester sauce. Cover and simmer for 20 minutes. Add yoghurt and stir in well. Add the tomatoes and cook gently for 15 minutes more until the tomatoes are heated through. Serve with rice.

Though desserts are most likely to be a piece of the many varieties of fresh fruit available in the Algarve or just a juicy orange, for a special dinner ending, this Regua Cream, a recipe from the north, is quickly cooked over hot water on the stove top. It is a Portuguese variation of zabaglione — creamier and a soft rich pudding.

Regua Cream

(Creme a moda de regua)

125g/4oz sugar
150ml/¹/₄ pint milk

3 or 4 egg-yolks

Mix sugar and milk together and blend in the egg-yolks. Heat the mixture gently till it becomes thick in a double boiler (or a bowl in a pan of boiling water), stirring well all the time. Serve hot, sprinkled with grated chocolate (cheat by crumbling something like a Cadbury's Flake bar if available).

Using port, the flavour of strawberries can be enhanced in this classic dish.

Fraises Romanoff
(Morangas a moda de Romanoff)

*30ml/2 tablespoons each
vanilla ice cream and
whipped cream*

*½kg/1lb strawberries
2 glasses tawny port*

Soak the strawberries for an hour in port and, just before serving, add the ice cream and whipped cream.

9

MEALS FOR FOUR TO SIX

Family meals Portuguese-style tend to be leisurely affairs perhaps taken a little later in the day than here. The same can apply in a self-catering situation with emphasis placed on dinner as the main meal or perhaps one can entertain other couples at their villa or apartment, part of the fun of having one's 'own place' for the holiday.

The following recipes are fairly substantial and nourishing in the Portuguese manner and most are suitable to serve at any time of the year.

The Portuguese love soups and two contrasting ones from very different regions of the country are *caldo verde*, the cabbage soup of the north which has now become a national dish, and *gazpacho*, from the hotter Alentejo borderlands with Spain. This soup is not solely Spanish; the Portuguese have their own version with characteristic additional touches of a slice of *chourico* sausage or chopped ham. It is the perfect soup to serve outdoors on a hot day.

Note: unless otherwise stated, all the recipes in this section serve 4 people.

Green cabbage soup
(Caldo verde)

450g/1 lb potatoes
450g/1 lb cabbage
1 large onion
seasoning

slice of Continental-style
  sausage
15ml/1 tablespoon olive oil
  (optional)

Boil potatoes in salted water (chicken stock will give the soup added flavour). When cooked, blend to a purée and reheat. When the mixture is boiling, add finely shredded cabbage (see pages 18 and 24) and seasoning. For the best flavour add the cabbage 10-15 minutes before serving. Portuguese cooks will add a slice of sausage and chopped onion or a tablespoon of olive oil for each of 4 servings to the potato mixture. In the north of Portugal, the soup is served with a thick piece of maize bread.

Alentejo gazpacho

88g/3½oz bread
450g/1lb tomatoes
2 green peppers
2 garlic cloves
45ml/3 tablespoons olive oil
½ cucumber

22ml/1½ tablespoons
   vinegar
salt, pepper
sliced Continental-style
   sausage (optional)
chopped ham (optional)

Cut the bread in thin slices and small cubes and brown slightly in the oven. Skin the tomatoes, remove seeds and cut in small pieces. Cut the green peppers in slices. Crush the tomatoes, peppers, garlic, salt and toasted bread together to make a pulp. Add olive oil, pepper and vinegar. Put in a large bowl and soak, preferably for a day, in a cool place. Add sliced cucumber, some fresh sliced green pepper and tomatoes as a garnish and cubed pieces of toasted bread before serving. Add sliced sausage and chopped ham to give a Portuguese touch.

In case you want the conversation piece interest of 'When I cooked octopus in Portugal' this recipe will guide you. In fact octopus is reasonably cheap at 200-300 *escudos* a kilo and cooked gently need not be chewy and unappetising.

Octopus rice

(Arroz de polvo)

1 octopus
200ml/7½ fl. oz red wine
163ml/5¼ fl. oz olive oil
1 onion
2 garlic cloves

3 tomatoes
1 green pepper
350g/12oz rice
salt, pepper
piri piri

Cook the prepared octopus in a little water with the red wine. Cut the octopus in small slices and keep the cooking liquid.

Cook together, slowly and stirring often, the olive oil, onion, and finely chopped garlic, skinned and deseeded tomatoes cut in pieces, and the green pepper cut in lengthwise slices. Season with salt, pepper and piri piri sauce (see page 18) to taste. This when cooked makes the *refogado* or basic sauce. Take three times the amount of cooking water of the octopus and add it to the sauce. Bring to the boil. Season to taste and add the washed rice. When it is again boiling, lower the heat so that it cooks slowly; the rice when ready should be quite damp. This is an Algarvean recipe and at the fishmarket ask for the octopus to be prepared. Don't buy a small one which shrinks after cooking and never salt the octopus before it is cooked or it becomes hard. It will also become hard if you cook it for too long.

Clams are sold in plastic bags in freezer compartments of supermarkets and should be well washed till all the grit has gone before being used. A clam sauce (which can be made more easily with a tin of clams also available in shops) goes well with spaghetti for a quick supper dish for the family.

Spaghetti with clam sauce
(Spaghetti com molho ameijoas)

350g/12oz spaghetti or
   tagliatelle
275g/10oz canned clams
150g/5oz × 2 cans of
   tomato purée
1 finely chopped onion

15ml/1 tablespoon oil
5ml/1 teaspoon mixed herbs
30ml/2 tablespoons white
   wine
seasoning

Cook the pasta in plenty of boiling salted water until tender or *al dente*. Drain. Meanwhile soften the chopped onion in oil in a saucepan. Drain the clams and add to the onion together with the tomato purée, herbs and white wine. Season to taste and mix all the ingredients together. When the sauce is heated through, serve the pasta and top with the clam sauce.

Clams in their shells (which cost from 120-600 *escudos* a kilo) can be cooked with pork Algarve-style using a pan rather than the traditional *cataplana*.

Pork with clams
(Porco e ameijoas)

450g/1lb pork loin
1kg/2lb clams
4-5 garlic cloves
30ml/2 tablespoons pork fat
15ml/1 tablespoon olive oil

sprig parsley
15ml/1 tablespoon flour
1 lemon
salt

Heat the olive oil and pork fat together and when very hot fry the meat cut in small pieces in it little by little. Season lightly with salt. When cooked put meat on one side and continue frying till all the meat is cooked. Peel the garlic cloves, leaving on the last pink skin, and add, slightly crushed, to the last of the meat to be cooked, with the parsley torn into small pieces by hand. Stir, sprinkle with flour and fry for a few minutes. Wash clams very well and add to the pan. Raise the heat to evaporate some of the liquid while the clams open. Add the rest of the cooked meat and cook all together for a few minutes. Season if necessary. Sprinkle with lemon juice and serve immediately with fried potatoes.

Pork is the most available of Portuguese meats. In this recipe, the popular Portuguese flavours of orange and caramel are mixed in for an unusual taste combination.

Pork escalopes with orange and caramel sauce
(Carne de porco com molito do laranja)

45ml/3 tablespoons oil
1 small finely chopped onion
125g/4oz cup mushrooms,
    wiped and finely chopped
30ml/2 tablespoons
    chopped fresh parsley
salt, pepper
4 × 75g/3oz pork escalopes

30ml/2 tablespoons
    granulated sugar
15ml/1 tablespoon water
15ml/1 tablespoon vinegar
150ml/1/4 pint chicken stock
1 orange
10ml/2 teaspoons cornflour

Stir the sugar in a saucepan over a moderate heat until the sugar has dissolved and turned caramel in colour. Draw the pan off the heat at once and add the water and vinegar (be careful as the liquid will cause the sugar to boil up). Return to the heat and stir to dissolve the caramel. Stir in the stock. Peel the orange thinly and cut the peel into very thin strips.

Stir into the pan and simmer gently for 20 minutes. Blend the cornflour with the orange juice, stir into the sauce, bring to the boil and cook for one minute. Heat 15ml/1 tablespoon oil then fry the onion until soft. Add the mushrooms and cook for a further 2 minutes. Stir in parsley and seasoning. Flatten escalopes between two sheets of greaseproof paper. Divide mushroom mixture between the escalopes, roll up and secure with cocktail sticks. Heat the remaining oil in a frying pan then cook escalopes for about 15 minutes, turning them occasionally. Reheat the sauce and serve with the escalopes.

If you want to try cooking the dry cod, *bacalhau*, this recipe is very popular and served in the Sheraton Lisbon hotel.

Baked cod Sheraton
(Bacalhau a lagareiro)
(Serves 6)

4 portions of codfish	1 lemon
(*bacalhau*): 600g/22oz	2 eggs
175ml/6 fl. oz milk	dry bread
4 garlic cloves	50g/2oz butter
salt, pepper	350ml/12 fl. oz olive oil

Cut the cod in big pieces and the day before it is needed put it in water. Change in water two or three times within the 24 hours of soaking. Two hours before starting to cook, dry the *bacalhau*. Cover it with the milk, slices of garlic, salt, pepper and lemon juice. Later dry the *bacalhau* pieces and dip them in the beaten eggs and then in the dry bread crushed into breadcrumbs. Place the cod in an earthenware pan and place a little butter on each piece. Pour the olive oil into the pan (without covering the cod) together with two soup spoons of the milk marinade. Put the pan in the oven and baste the cod with the sauce from time to time. Cook in a medium oven till the cod is very hot and well cooked; drain and serve with boiled potatoes and a green salad.

Sole is a popular fish particularly in Lisbon and this is a quick and tasty way of cooking sole fillets though all kinds of small fish can be cooked in the same way. Mackerel and sardines can also be treated in the same manner.

Sole Vila Franca (serves 4-6)

(Linguado a moda de Vila Franca)

1kg/2lb sole fillets	*oil*
1 glass milk	*salt, pepper*
1 lemon	*vegetable oil to taste*
flour	*1kg/2lb potatoes*
olive	

Prepare the fish and soak in cold milk and salt for at least 15 minutes. Remove and dry. Dust with flour on both sides and fry fish in hot olive oil till golden and crisp. Dry again in a kitchen towel and season with salt and pepper. Serve with slices of lemon and chipped potatoes.

Chicken is easily available, costs about 275 *escudos* a kilo and can be used in these two Portuguese ways.

Jugged chicken and rice

(Arroz de frango de cabidela)

1 jointed chicken	*½ garlic sausage* (chourico)
275g/10oz rice	*cut in slices*
45ml/3 tablespoons olive oil	*15ml/1 tablespoon vinegar*
2 large chopped onions	*salt to taste*
1 sprig parsley	*1 litre/2 pints stock*

Put oil, chicken joints, onions, chopped parsley, sausage, salt and stock in a large pan. Bring to the boil, add rice and simmer. Add any chicken blood (mixed with vinegar to prevent it congealing), stirring well. Cook gently over a low heat till the chicken is tender. In Portugal the rice is served separately after, draining well.

Chicken a Castelo Vide (for 4-6)

(Frango a Castelo Vide)

1 boiling chicken (2-3kg/4-6lb)	*125g/4oz butter*
	3 egg-yolks
bouquet garni of onions	*4-6 large blanched and*
bay leaf, celery ends, carrot	*skinned tomatoes*
225g/8oz rice	*125g/4oz sliced button*
sprig of parsley	*mushrooms*

Boil the chicken with the bouquet garni. Remove and put on one side when cooked. Boil the rice in the chicken stock for 20 minutes and then strain. Remove chicken meat from the bone while still warm and cut into bite-sized pieces. Place tomatoes in the bottom of a casserole around the edge and put the chicken meat in the centre with raw sliced mushrooms on top. Cover with rice and dot with pieces of butter. Beat together the egg-yolks and pour over the rice. Cover and bake in a moderate oven (180C/350F/Gas mark 4) till the eggs are set.

Rabbit is found in the Algarve and is stewed with local wine and tomatoes. These two stew versions make the most of this under-rated meat.

Stewed rabbit a Porcalhota
(Coelho em vinho)

1 rabbit (about 1kg/2lb)
125ml/4 fl. oz white or red
   wine
225ml/8 fl oz stock
30ml/2 tablespoons tomato
   purée or 4 tomatoes
45ml/3 tablespoons olive oil

10ml/2 teaspoons fat or
   butter
1 large chopped onion
1 garlic clove
10ml/2 teaspoons chopped
   parsley
salt, pepper

Skin, clean and joint the rabbit (keep all the blood). Seal joints in fat in a pan. Place meat in the bottom of a large pan without the pieces touching each other. Cover with wine, stock and olive oil, tomatoes, onions, salt, pepper, parsley and the blood. Cook over a medium heat for an hour or more till the meat is tender.

Porches rabbit stew
(Coelho a moda de Porches)

1 rabbit (1-1½kg/2-3lb)
   jointed
15ml/1 tablespoon oil
25g/1oz margarine
1 chopped onion
22ml/1½ tablespoons
   cornflour

150ml/¼ pint white wine
450g/1lb sliced tomatoes
275ml/½ pint stock
salt, pepper
450g/1lb potatoes peeled
   chopped or sliced

Soak the rabbit joints in cold salted water for several hours. Drain and dry well. Heat the oil and margarine in a flameproof casserole. Fry the rabbit and onions till lightly browned. Sprinkle cornflour in, stir and cook for 1 minute. Stir in the wine and allow to bubble for a few seconds. Add the stock, tomatoes and seasoning. Bring to the boil, cover well and simmer for 1-1½ hours. Add potatoes for the last 30 minutes.

Puddings are often loved by children who will probably fall for the sweet custards of the Portuguese. Though the cook will not want to spend too much time making them, the following can be prepared as special meal treats or if dining more formally.

Pudim flan

(this version comes from Moncao in northern Portugal)

450g/1lb sugar   *575ml/1 pint water*
grated lemon rind   *6 eggs*

Mix the sugar and water and boil slowly till a thick syrup is formed. Make sure the sugar is dissolved before the water boils to avoid crystallisation. Allow to cool, add lemon peel and well-beaten eggs. Cook gently on a low heat or in a double boiler. Stir till the mixture becomes thick and creamy or custard-like. Serve cold with sponge fingers or wafer biscuits.

Pudim Molotov

4 eggs   *1 small glass port*
200g/7oz sugar   *juice of ¼ lemon*

Grease a mould (preferably one with a hole in the middle) and dust with sugar. Separate the eggs and whisk whites till stiff. Add half the sugar, beating all the time. Add a few drops of lemon juice and beat again. Fill the mould with the mixture and bake in a *bain-marie* (place the mould in a roasting tin three quarters full of water) for about an hour in a medium oven (180C/350F/Gas mark 4) with the mould covered. Turn out the pudding and allow to cool. Prepare a sauce by mixing well the egg-yolks and the rest of the sugar with a wooden spoon; add the port. While still stirring, heat gently, taking care not to burn the mixture or turn it lumpy. When the mixture thickens and goes creamy, remove it from the heat and allow to cool. Pour sauce over the pudding and serve.

Though not a Portuguese recipe, this idea has the Portuguese love of mixing bread and spice for a dessert (see Rabanadas on page 107) and uses the traditional sweet flavourings of cinnamon and orange. It is a good way of using up stale bread.

Sweet orange panperdy
(Omeleta com laranja)

125g/4oz butter
6 slices cubed white bread
30ml/2 tablespoons brown
    sugar mixed with a little
    cinnamon
6 large eggs

30ml/2 tablespoons caster
    sugar
grated rind and flesh of 2
    oranges
icing sugar to dust

Heat 25g/1oz of butter and toss the bread cubes in it in a pan till golden brown and crisp. Remove from the pan and toss in brown sugar and cinnamon. Beat the eggs, sugar and orange rind together. Melt the rest of the butter in a pan. Pour egg mixture into the pan and cook over a moderate heat until the underneath is set. Divide oranges into segments removing all the pith. Place oranges and bread cubes over half the omelette, fold in half and slide onto a plate. Dust with icing sugar and serve immediately. If you do not have a very large pan to make an omelette big enough for four, divide the mixture in half and cook as for two separate omelettes.

Santa Clara mould (serves 4-6)
(Doce a moda de Santa Clara)

450g/1lb large prunes
62$\frac{1}{2}$g/2$\frac{1}{2}$oz demerara
    sugar
$\frac{1}{2}$ bottle ruby port

juice of $\frac{1}{2}$ lemon
30ml/2 tablespoons
    powdered gelatine
275ml/$\frac{1}{2}$ pint cream

Sprinkle the sugar over the prunes in a bowl and soak overnight in the port and lemon juice. Stone the prunes and poach them gently in the port marinade. Blend to a purée, stir in gelatine dissolved in a little water. Place in a ring or other mould and leave to set. Turn out and fill the centre or decorate with whipped cream.

10

MEALS FOR LARGER GROUPS

The larger of Portugal's rentable villas, particularly in the Algarve, come often with their own swimming pool, maid/ cook, more extensive garden with, perhaps, even a tennis court. It makes economic sense for this touch of stylish living for friends to join up or create a family get-together forming groups of 10 or 12 to hire a single villa. Kitchen and cooking chores can be cut down by asking each couple or family to cope for an equal share of the holiday days with shopping being done jointly and costs being equalled out.

The following recipes are for those who need to cook comforting soups and stews for several appetites or who want to create casual outdoor buffets and barbecue fare for their own groups and invited friends. The charm of most of these recipes is that the oven hardly needs to be used. One can cook in the huge pans the Portuguese favour on top of the stove, in a big *cataplana* or over the barbecue.

Many of the large villas or apartment complexes have their own barbecue area. If not, you can buy a *fogareiro* (see page 62) and set up a barbecue where you wish. With wire holders for easier grilling, an enjoyable barbecue can be set up on the beach or in the patio. You can study the tech- niques in some of the beach restaurants where the family cooks fish over these small barbecues at the back and serves it quickly and simply to the guests at table.

Sardines are often very cheap: 50-100 *escudos* a kilo. The fish are rich and nourishing in natural oils so can be grilled with no further cooking oil additions, though to prevent them sticking it is best to brush the grill with oil before cooking. Clean small fish by pulling out the guts through a small in- cision through the gills. Wash through with cold water. Larger sardines can be split down the back, opened out and boned.

Herbs (especially mint) can be used to stuff or scatter on opened fish. Cook sardines quickly on a fast flame. Serve with lemon juice and to make a bigger meal, with the *Alentejo acorda* soup (see below) and green salads, not forgetting lots of chilled *vinho verde* wine. Hunks of crusty bread, rice or boiled potatoes are other ideal sardine partners.

Soups are a wonderful way of using up scraps of foods and clearing the store cupboard at the end of a self-catering holiday and are quick to serve.

Alentejo bread soup (serves 6-8)
(Acorda)

The wheat-producing area north-east of the Algarve, the Alentejo, has traditional bread soups in which their staple foodstuff replaces or stretches vegetables and meat. More or less anything can be added — scraps of meat or game. This one is very nourishing but only uses herbs, olive oil, bread and water to achieve its effect. It goes well as an accompaniment to grilled sardines and is a wonderful store cupboard clearer of stale bread. Quick to make and, apart from boiling some water, needs no cooking.

1 small bunch fresh coriander	42ml/2¾ tablespoons olive oil
3-4 cloves garlic	250g/9oz stale bread
1¾ litre/3½ pints water	salt

Pound the coriander, salt and garlic to a paste. Place in a large serving bowl, add olive oil, stirring well, then pour in boiling water and add the bread torn in small pieces. Mix well till smooth and serve at once.

Watercress soup (serves 6)
(Sopa de agriões)

2 bunches watercress	¼ litre/½ pint milk
6 potatoes, medium-size, sliced	50g/2oz butter
2 egg-yolks	1 onion
	salt

Remove leaves from watercress stalks, wash and put on one

side. Boil the potatoes with chopped watercress stalks and chopped onion. When cooked, sieve or blend till smooth. Add chopped watercress leaves and salt to taste. Cook with the lid off the pan for 15 minutes. Add the butter and, when it has melted, add the egg-yolks beaten with the milk. Reheat (but do not allow to boil) and serve at once.

Canja (serves 8)

a classic Portuguese chicken soup

6 cups chicken stock　　　*275g/10oz rice*
225g/8oz fat bacon or ham,　*seasoning*
*　chopped*

Cook the bacon gently in the chicken stock. Add seasoning and rice. When the rice is cooked through, serve the soup.

Canja is the term applied to all kinds of chicken broth in Portugal. Rice and ham are the common ingredients but chopped roast chestnuts, lemon juice, egg-yolks, onion and nutmeg may be added. In some regions, fresh mint is added, which gives a lovely summery taste and can be combined with lemon juice flavouring. Allow about 12ml/^{3}/$_4$ tablespoon fresh chopped mint per person and add just before serving or it loses its impact.

Fisherman's soup (serves 8)

(Sopa a pescador)

Variations on this kind of soup are found all over Portugal. This one has an Algarvean touch (which originally came from the chef at the Eva hotel at Faro) of adding locally grown almonds to the soup.

2 large onions　　　　*2 litres/4 pints fish stock*
garlic　　　　　　　*450g/1lb flaked almonds*
4 tomatoes　　　　　*60ml/4 tablespoons olive oil*
1kg/2lb crayfish　　　*225g/8oz rice*
*　(langoustines)*　　　*chopped parsley*

Fry the chopped onion with chopped garlic in olive oil till golden. Chop the tomatoes and shelled crayfish (big prawns or other shellfish can be substituted). Add fish stock, finely chopped garlic and flaked almonds all together in a big pan and boil gently for about 45 minutes. The rice should be added after about 30 minutes. Add chopped parsley just before serving.

Out of doors in the garden or by the pool, lighter cold food is usually the requirement. These hors d'oeuvres ideas can be padded out with salads and chunks of fresh baked bread for lunch or made part of an evening barbecue buffet.

Tuna fish paté

(Empadinha)

Blend equal amounts of tinned tuna with butter. Season with a little piri piri sauce (see page 18), salt, pepper, Worcester sauce if available, mustard and half a liqueur glass each of port and brandy. Chill slightly before serving. Tuna can also be used fresh-cooked or tinned for a salad or a spread.

Tuna and apple salad (serves 8)

(Salada de atum e maça)

4 × 400g/14oz tins tuna
4 green eating apples, cored and chopped
8 sticks celery
8 tomatoes
275ml/½ pint mayonnaise or natural yoghurt
salt, pepper

Drain and flake the tuna. Place in a large bowl with the apples, chopped celery and tomatoes. Stir in the mayonnaise or yoghurt. Season to taste. Serve with crisp lettuce and cucumber.

Tuna avocado spread

(Pasta com atum) Makes about 575ml/1 pint

200g/7oz tin of tuna
1 avocado
15ml/1 tablespoon lemon juice
15ml/1 tablespoon olive or salad oil
1 finely chopped garlic clove
7½ml/1½ teaspoons grated onion
2½ml/½ teaspoon salt
4 drops Tabasco (or piri piri sauce)

Drain and flake tuna. Peel avocado and remove stone. Grate avocado using a medium grater. Mix all the ingredients lightly together and serve on toast or cracker biscuits.

Tuna bread
(Pao com atum)

This picnic or lunch buffet idea was described to me by Luis Cancella de Abreu of the Portuguese Tourist Office in Lisbon. It is one he especially liked as a child. Mix 2-3 tins of tuna and one of anchovies with milk, stoneless olives (black and green), mayonnaise, olive oil (or vegetable oil), chopped tomatoes, chopped chives and herbs to taste, with the soft crumbs from the hollowed-out inside of a large tin loaf of bread to make a fairly stiff paste. Fill the hollowed-out loaf with the mixture and chill for a while in the fridge. Serve with a mixed salad.

Ovos verdes
(a green filling for hard-boiled eggs)

For filling every two eggs you need:

5ml/1 teaspoon minced onion
5ml/1 teaspoon (scant) curry powder
15ml/1 tablespoon mayonnaise

15ml-plus/1 heaped tablespoon finely chopped parsley

Boil the eggs for 10 minutes. Place in cold water for 10 minutes and then remove shells. Cut in half lengthways and ease out the yolks. Mash the yolks with all the above ingredients. Pile back into the egg-whites and serve mixed with black olives, radishes and spring onions as an hors d'oeuvre or appetiser.

Tomatoes recheados

Slice off the tops of tomatoes, scoop the insides out and fill with crumbled stale bread mixed with grated cheese (Parmesan is ideal). Mix half and half with the chopped, scooped-out tomato and season with salt and pepper. Put a dab of butter on the top. Replace the tomato tops and bake in the oven until tender with 30ml/2 tablespoons olive oil poured over them. Serve with barbecue and other meats, or on their own as a hot meal opener.

Rice does not have to be served hot and these two ideas

use the local rice grown in Portugal with local fish to make a sustaining cold salad dish.

Tuna fish rice

(Arroz de atum)

Wash cold cooked rice. Mix with mayonnaise, tuna and chopped lettuce and tomato in a large pudding basin. Press down hard and turn out to form a mould. Decorate with olives and chopped hard-boiled egg. Chill well until served. This makes an effective and easy buffet centrepiece with little equipment or effort. It makes a good lunch dish served with different salads.

Fish and rice salad

(Salada de peixe e arroz)
Serves 8; can also be served cold

1kg/2lb fish fillets
450g/1lb rice
2 crushed garlic cloves
   (optional)
30ml/2 tablespoons white
   wine vinegar
8 medium tomatoes

120ml/8 tablespoons olive
   oil
salt, pepper
2 red peppers
8 spring onions
2 small cans sweetcorn

Steam the fish, allow to cool and flake. Cook rice, rinse well and leave to cool. Mix the garlic, olive oil, vinegar and seasoning. Seed and chop peppers. Chop tomatoes and spring onions. Mix fish, rice and vegetables and pour over the vinegar oil dressing. Serve chilled.

Patio pizza

The flavoursome tomatoes, herbs, black olives and garlic sausage of Portugal can be used in an Italian way to create a holiday pizza made all in one in a large frying pan and sliced and served hot or cold as a meal opener or with an aperitif and as a lunch with a salad.

For the scone dough:
175g/6oz self raising flour
2.5ml/^{1}/$_2$ teaspoon salt
50g/2oz margarine or butter

90-105ml/6-7 tablespoons
   milk

For the topping:

30ml/2 tablespoons tomato
   purée or ketchup
125g/4oz thinly sliced garlic
   sausage

3 large sliced tomatoes
50g/2oz grated cheese
pinch fresh herbs
salt, pepper

Mix flour and salt in a bowl, rub in the fat till it resembles fine breadcrumbs. Stir in the milk to form a soft dough. Roll out to a 25cm/10-inch round and grease a big enough frying pan. Press the dough into the pan and cover the pan. Cook very slowly over a low heat without removing the cover for about 10-15 minutes till the dough has risen. Spread ketchup or purée over the dough with the back of a spoon. Arrange the sausage on top with the sliced tomatoes. Sprinkle with cheese, herbs, salt and pepper. Place under a hot grill for 4-5 minutes till the cheese is golden and bubbling.

A big stew whether of meat (cozido) or fish (caldeirada) makes a sustaining party dish or will feed large numbers on a cooler day. The caldeirada is found all over Portugal and varies according to the local fish available. Little bags of fish pieces ready to make the stew can be found in the fish markets to ease the ingredients list. Squid can be used as an optional addition and the use of fillets is quicker as the bones do not have to be removed but this makes the dish more expensive to make. The best flavour will result, of course, if the fish used is fresh.

Caldeirada
Serves 8

1½kg/3lb mixed fish
4 onions
400g/1lb clams in their
   shells
6 garlic cloves

salt, pepper
paprika to taste
olive oil for cooking
sliced stale bread
parsley

Slice the onions in a large pan. Add chopped garlic, salt and pepper, paprika, chopped parsley and oil. Fry for a few minutes. Add water to cover the fish cut in pieces. Add the clams. Chopped tomatoes can be added with the onions. Heat through till the clams open and everything is cooked. Serve with fried bread pieces.

Meat stew
(Cozido a Portuguesa)

1kg/2lb shin of beef
225g/8oz streaky bacon
1kg/2lb potatoes
450g/1lb carrots

450g/1lb turnips
1 large cabbage
1 smoked sausage
350g/12oz rice

Put the meat in a large pan of boiling water. Add the bacon and simmer slowly. After about 2 hours add peeled potatoes, carrots, turnips and cabbage cut in quarters. When the vegetables are half cooked, add slices of smoked sausage. Remove some of the liquid and use to cook the rice separately. When everything is cooked, serve the stew in a large dish with the meat in the centre and vegetables around it. The rice is served in a separate dish. The liquid in which everything has been cooked is an excellent soup on its own. Traditionally, the Portuguese serve the meat and vegetables set out on a huge platter in separate little mounds.

The Portuguese are fond of steamed meat and seasonings cooked together. For chicken the bland flesh is steamed with mustard, port and brandy. Though the Portuguese use whole chicken, jointed portions are equally good and easier to manage.

Chicken in the pot
(Frango na pucara)

2 small chicken or 8 good
joints
4 medium chopped
tomatoes
175g/6oz chopped smoked
ham
12 small chopped onions or
shallots

125g/4oz butter
4 crushed or finely chopped
garlic cloves
2 wine glasses port
2 wine glasses brandy
30ml/2 tablespoons mustard
white wine to taste
salt, pepper

Place all the ingredients in a large casserole or earthenware pot. Cover and cook slowly on top of the stove till the chicken is cooked. Remove the lid and let the top brown a little. Serve with fried potatoes and a mixed salad. In Portugal this dish is traditionally cooked in a tall earthenware pot (on sale everywhere), but any big thick pan with a lid would do.

Beira chicken
(Frango a moda de Beira) Serves 8

The Beiras are regions north of Lisbon around Coimbra with a long straight coastline. This chicken dish, cooked on top of the stove, has a rich sauce based on beaten egg-yolks. Again chicken joints rather than the whole bird will be easier to manage.

2 small chickens or 8 joints
50g/2oz butter
125g/4oz cooking fat
450g/1lb onions
4 egg-yolks
parsley

165ml/11 tablespoons white wine
juice of 2 lemons
575ml/1 pint stock
salt, pepper

Fry the chicken pieces (trimmed and jointed from the whole chicken) in butter and cooking fat in a deep pan. When golden brown, add the wine, stock, pepper, salt and roughly chopped or halved onions. Simmer gently on top of the stove till the chicken is cooked. Drain off the liquid and add beaten egg-yolks, chopped parsley and lemon juice. Mix well and pour this sauce over the chicken. Serve with fried potatoes.

Lamb is a somewhat scarce meat in Portugal but lamb meat can go further and gains flavour from being cooked over a barbecue as kebabs. The marinade here uses honey, local wine and olive oil with spices.

Lamb and mushroom kebabs
(Anho assado no espeto com cogumelos) Makes 6 kebabs

700g/1½lb lamb (from the leg)
225g/8oz button mushrooms
1 red pepper
1 green pepper
fresh bay leaves
For the marinade:
30ml/2 tablespoons clear honey

90ml/6 tablespoons red wine
90ml/6 tablespoons olive oil
crushed garlic clove
salt, pepper
4 drops chilli sauce (or piri piri sauce)
For the sauce:
5ml/1 teaspoon cornflour
cold water

Put honey in a large bowl after it has been gently warmed. Stir in rest of the marinade ingredients. Cut lamb in cubes; wipe mushrooms. Deseed and chop peppers into 2.5cm/1-inch pieces. Thread lamb, vegetables and bay leaves onto six kebab skewers and place in a large shallow dish. Brush marinade over and leave to soak for 2 hours, turning occasionally. Cook under the grill or over a barbecue, basting with the marinade as necessary. Make a sauce from 5ml/1 teaspoon cornflour blended with a little cold water. Blend in marinade and any cooking juices from the kebabs. Stir well over a high heat, then lower heat and cook gently, stirring till sauce thickens. Season to taste and add a little extra wine if necessary. Serve the wine sauce with the kebabs.

Do not be put off by the title of this recipe. The Portuguese version of rissoles is light and crispy and excellent as a light snack with drinks or to eat with a salad.

Rissoles
(Rissois) Makes 24

For the pastry:
425ml/³⁄4 pint water
50g/2oz butter
275g/10oz plain flour
5ml/1 teaspoon salt

For the coating:
2 beaten eggs
175g/6oz fresh white
    breadcrumbs
oil for deep frying

For the filling:
50g/2oz butter
50g/2oz plain flour
425ml/³⁄4 pint milk
225g/8oz prawns, chopped
salt, pepper
30ml/2 tablespoons lemon
    juice
15ml/1 tablespoon chopped
    parsley

To make the pastry mix flour and salt. Bring water to the boil with the butter. When the butter has melted tip in the flour and mix well. Remove from the heat beating quickly until the mixture leaves the sides of the pan. Turn the mixture out onto a floured plate, cover with cling-film and leave to cool. To make the filling, melt butter in a pan, add flour and cook for 1 minute, stirring to mix well. Remove from heat and gradually add the milk. Bring to the boil, stirring, until thickened. Remove from the heat, add prawns, salt, pepper, lemon juice and parsley. Cool. Roll out pastry thinly and cut into 24 × 10cm/4-inch rounds. Place a little filling in the centre of each round. Brush the edge of the pastry with water, then fold over the dough. Press to seal. Coat with beaten egg and cover with breadcrumbs. Chill for 30 minutes. Heat oil to 180°C/360°F and fry rissoles until golden brown, which takes about 3 minutes. Serve warm.

Probably the easiest dessert for a lot of people — and one of the most refreshing — is an orange salad. This is a recipe I picked up in a hotel at the fishing village of Nazare on the west coast.

Orange salad
(Salada de laranjas)

Allow one large orange per person. Peel and slice thinly. Place in a large dish with sugar to taste and any juice. Add (per 5 people) ½ liqueur glass of each of the following: brandy, port, whisky. Stir and chill well. This is very throat-cleansing after pork or sardine dishes.

Strawberries can also be treated with port and sugar. Pour a little dry port over strawberries in a bowl and leave to marinate for an hour or two. Add a few peeled slices of orange and a little sugar to taste.

If you want to show off with a typical Portuguese pudding or sweetmeat that can be served with coffee or tea mid-morning or afternoon if friends come round, here are some to try.

Golden soup
(Sopa dorada) Serves 8-10

200g/7oz bread (with crusts removed)
87g/3½oz butter for frying
487g/17½oz sugar

10 egg-yolks
87g/3½ chopped peeled almonds
cinnamon powder

Cut the bread into cubes and fry in butter. Add sugar and heat till the sugar is hot enough to make a thread when dipped in cold water. Remove from the heat and allow to cool a little. Add beaten egg-yolks and almonds and beat well. Return to the heat to thicken if necessary (but do not allow to boil). Place in a serving dish and scatter the surface with a little cinnamon powder.

Egg and almond pudding
(Pudim flan a moda de Maria Emilia) Serves 6-8

This family recipe was described to me by Lisbon cookery expert Mrs Maria Emilia Cancella de Abreu.

500g/18oz sugar
125g/4oz almonds without their skins
20 egg-yolks
5ml/1 teaspoon cinnamon

125g/4oz cidrao, preserved lemon pieces (crystallised candied lemon peel would do)
butter and sugar for cooking

Boil the sugar with water to make a syrup till the 'soft ball stage' is reached. Leave to cool. Chop almonds finely (or use ground almonds) and grate lemon pieces. Mix these with the beaten egg-yolks and cinnamon. Place the mixture in a mould in a *bain-marie* and cook in a low oven for 1 hour. Serve with the syrup.

Sonhos
(Dreams)

A traditional dessert recipe which Filipa Vacondeus described to me after she had made 5 dozen 'dreams' on a TV programme in Lisbon.

213ml/7½ fl. oz water
213g/7½oz self-raising flour
4 eggs
15ml/1 tablespoon margarine or butter
vegetable oil for deep frying

For the syrup:
250g/9oz sugar
87ml/3½fl. oz water
zest of 1 lemon
small cinnamon stick

Mix all the ingredients together and with two teaspoons make little rounds. Deep-fry in plenty of oil (not too hot or the pieces won't become bigger). Prick the rounds with a fork to aid the expansion and lightness. Cook till light and golden in batches of 12 or so for about an hour. Make a syrup using icing or ordinary sugar on the basis of 250g/9oz sugar to 87ml/3½ fl. oz water boiled with lemon zest and a cinnamon stick. Remove 'dreams' from oil, drain well on kitchen paper and serve coated with the syrup sauce (remove the cinnamon stick).

Another idea from Filipa Vacondeous is to use up the inevitable accumulation of egg-whites that occur when making the *pudim* flan-style recipes (particularly like the egg and almond pudding above). Chocolate mousse is understandably a popular dessert in Portugal.

Chocolate mousse
(Mousse chocolate a Filipa) Serves 6-8

60ml/4 tablespoons
    unsweetened chocolate
    powder (cacao)
	4 egg-whites
	60ml/4 tablespoons sugar

Beat together the egg-whites till stiff and fold in sugar and chocolate powder. Place this in the fridge to set.

Toucinhos

Toucinhos is the word for bacon but here refers to a very Algarvean dessert which should be set in little 5cm/2-inch small cake patty tins which can be used partly filled. The finished texture should be yellow and shiny surfaced. Makes about 20.

400g/14oz sugar *just over 275ml/¹/₂ pint* *water*	*2 egg whites* *20ml/2 dessert spoons flour* *7 egg-yolks*

For the syrup sauce, boil the sugar and water together till the sugar dissolves (stir for about 5 minutes). Pour into a *bain-marie* or double boiler filled with cold water to cool. Meanwhile beat egg-yolks and whites with flour and when sugar is cool mix with the eggs. Grease tiny moulds or patty tins and place mixture in these and cook in a *bain-marie* with water half way up the sides for about half an hour in a medium to low oven adding more water to the *bain-marie* as necessary. Serve with the syrup sauce.

To make the little Algarvean sweetmeats using local figs and almonds to serve with after-dinner coffee, you need a mincer or electric grinder. Here is a simple method to create a delightful mix of tastes.

Fig balls

(Bolas de figo) Makes about 675g/1½ lbs

105ml/7 tablespoons water
243g/8¾oz sugar
243g/8¾oz dried figs (stalks removed)
1 piece orange peel

243g/8¾oz peeled blanched almonds
43g/1¾oz cooking chocolate

Heat the almonds in the oven till roasted and lightly browned. Put almonds, figs, orange peel and chocolate together through a fine mincer or electric grinder. Boil the water with the sugar till thick and mix in the other ingredients. When cool form into little rounds and roll in sugar.

From the Alentejo district comes this recipe, again to serve as a sweetmeat after the meal.

Honey sweets

(Broas de mel)

488ml/17½oz honey
6 eggs
488ml/17½ fl. oz olive oil
15ml/1 tablespoon cinnamon

250g/9oz sugar
15ml/1 tablespoon aniseed
cornflour
plain flour
sugar crystals to coat

Beat well together the honey, olive oil, eggs, sugar, cinnamon and aniseed. Alternately add little by little both kinds of flour; the plain flour amounts to about ⅙ of the cornflour. The total quantity of flour depends on the size of the eggs used and the flour should be added till a rolling consistency of paste is obtained. Form the paste into small rounds and press each slightly with a fork so the lines stay visible. Bake in a hot oven till cooked (that is, when they have a fairly hard crust on the underneath side). When cooked, and while still hot, roll in sugar crystals (or granulated sugar will do). Makes about 30-40 sweets.

11

MENUS AND IDEAS FOR SPECIAL DIETS

Holidays in hotels can often pose problems for those with special dietary needs, whether medical, doctrinal, for slimmers or small children and babies. On a self-catering holiday, recipes and dietary needs can be adjusted as required.

Baby and dietary foods are available in supermarkets (see page 41) and those with special dietary needs can make their own choice among restaurant menus and shop ingredients to suit their needs. Rice and vegetable dishes will probably be the best in restaurants with salads and vegetable soups since there are few trends as yet towards vegetarianism in Portugal. But vegetarians cooking for themselves can take advantage of the wealth of good fresh produce adding rice and the nuts which are plentiful in the Algarve. Slimmers can stick to freshly grilled fish with fruit, avoid cooking in olive oil and forego the very sweet pastries and puddings. Portugal's diet is not a low calorie one. Take with you supplies of low-fat margarine and Gold or other favoured products.

The following recipes are in the main directed at vegetarians and those just wanting a lighter and healthy holiday diet with a few ideas for children.

Potato and runner bean soup

(Sopa de feijao verde a moda de Beira)
Serves 2-3; recipe from the Beira region

1 litre/2 pints water
1 onion
450g/1lb potatoes
82ml/5½ tablespoons olive
    oil

450g/1lb runner beans
225g/8oz tomatoes, peeled
    and seeded
salt

Boil the potatoes gently with the chopped onion, olive oil, tomatoes and salt in the water. Add more water if needed. Blend till smooth. Reheat and, as soon as the mixture starts to boil, add beans cut thinly and diagonally. Simmer till the beans are tender.

Another hearty soup that is almost a meal in itself comes from the old-established Reid's Hotel in Madeira.

Tomato and onion soup
(Sopa de tomate e cebola) Serves 4-5

1kg/2lb tomatoes	*25g/1oz butter*
1kg/2lb onions	*25g/1oz lard*
1 bay leaf	*25ml/1oz olive oil*
1 garlic clove	*4-5 eggs*
basil to taste	*75-125g/3-4oz grated*
2 slices bread and butter	*cheese*
salt, pepper	

Cut the onions in rounds and fry in olive oil, grated butter and lard, with the bay leaf and finely chopped garlic. Meanwhile put the tomatoes in boiling water briefly, remove the skins, cut in small pieces and add to the onions. Leave to cook for a few minutes with water to cover. Season to taste and add basil. Cut the bread in small pieces and place a few pieces in each soup bowl with some grated cheese (fried or toasted bread can be used as an alternative). Blend the tomatoes and onions to a puree, reheat and serve. A poached egg can be added, if wished, to each serving.

Aubergines are the base of these next two dishes to the first of which the non-vegetarian can add ham if wished.

Loulé market bake
(Legumes a moda de Loulé) Serves 4-6

450g/1lb thinly sliced aubergines	*10ml/2 teaspoons oregano*
	salt, pepper
15ml/1 tablespoon oil	*125g/4oz fresh white bread-crumbs*
450g/1lb chopped onions	
400g/14oz canned or fresh tomatoes	*125g/4oz grated cheese*
	175g/6oz slice cooked ham
5ml/1 teaspoon basil	*(optional)*

Put the aubergines in a pan with salt. Cover with boiling water and simmer for 2 minutes. Drain at once. Heat the oil in a frying pan, add the onions and cook till softened but not coloured. Add the tomatoes, herbs, seasoning and cook for about 10 minutes till the sauce is reduced by about one-third. Season to taste. Mix breadcrumbs and cheese together. Lightly oil a 1½ litre/2½ pint oven-proof dish. Make layers of the ingredients, putting half the aubergines on the base. Cover with half the tomato sauce, then a third of the crumb and cheese mix, and half the ham if used. Repeat the layers, ending with a third of the crumb and cheese mix. Cover with a lid or foil and bake at 190°C/375°F/Gas mark 5 for 40 minutes. Uncover the dish for the last 5 minutes to brown the top. Serve hot or cold with a green salad.

Algarve aubergines
(Beringela a Algarvia) Serves 4

4 small aubergines	60ml/4 tablespoons sweet
1 large onion	fortified wine (for
4 tomatoes	example, white port)
1 garlic clove	1 beaten egg
oil for frying	25g/1oz grated Parmesan
salt, pepper	cheese

Wash the aubergines and cut in half lengthways. Scoop out the flesh and chop finely. Keep the shells. Chop the onion and garlic finely. Fry gently in oil till golden. Add the aubergine flesh and fry for 5 minutes more. Meanwhile cover the tomatoes with boiling water and leave for 2 minutes. Drain, rinse in cold water and remove the skins. Chop and add to the aubergines. Mix with wine and salt and pepper to taste. Cover and simmer for 7-10 minutes till the aubergine is tender. Add beaten egg and stir over a low heat till the mixture is creamy, but do not allow to boil. Fill the aubergine shells with the mixture, sprinkle with cheese and reheat in the oven at 200°C/400°F/Gas mark 6 for 20 minutes. Serve with rice.

A Portuguese accompaniment to scrambled eggs uses vegetables cooked with a tomato sauce.

Tomatada a Portuguesa

Boil 3-4 kinds of vegetables (choose from potatoes, carrots, turnips, peas, green beans, cauliflower, broccoli, mushrooms, asparagus tips). When cooked, dice and mix vegetables together. Add 90-105ml/6-7 tablespoons tomato sauce according to taste. A basic tomato sauce that can be used here is described on page 18. Serve the *tomatada* hot with scrambled eggs.

Tomato rice
(Arroz de tomates) Serves 4

Typical of the way the Portuguese make rice as the base carrier for vegetables to make a filling tasty dish.

400g/14oz rice	88ml/3½ fl. oz olive oil or
4 medium tomatoes	50g/2oz lard
1 large onion	800ml/28 fl. oz stock/
salt, pepper	consommé

Make a *refogado* sauce (see page 19) by cooking chopped onion in olive oil or lard to fry. Add tomatoes without seeds, skinned and chopped finely. Fry till soft. Add stock, salt and pepper and bring to the boil. Add rice. Stir till cooked and soft. Continue to cook, with the pan covered on a low heat or in the oven till the rice mixture is dry.

Using frozen short-crust pastry and making a base as usual to line a pie dish, these two vegetable flan recipes are fine cold to take on picnics. They are from Mrs Maria Emilia Cancella de Abreu, who has 9 children and 12 grandchildren and is used to cooking for large groups.

Cauliflower pie
(Torta a couve-flor) Serves 4

Pastry base for flan tin lining (see below)

1 cauliflower	salt, pepper
3 egg-yolks and 1 egg-white	25g/1oz grated Parmesan
150ml/¼ pint cream	cheese

Boil the cauliflower till tender. Place in the pastry case and pour on the beaten eggs and cream seasoned to taste. Cook in a medium oven for 25 minutes and finish with grated Parmesan cheese browned in the oven or under the grill.

Spinach pie
(Torta a espinafres) Serves 4

Pastry base:
250g/9oz flour
125g/4oz butter
25g/1oz pork fat (lard)

1 egg
small spoonful milk

Mix all the ingredients together to make a dough. Roll out and shape to line a pie dish.

For the filling:
450g/1lb cooked spinach, chopped till smooth (do not purée in a machine)

300ml/¹/₂ pint cream
3 egg-yolks
25g/1oz Parmesan cheese
salt, pepper

Mix all the ingredients together, except the cheese, and place in the pie dish seasoned to taste and cook in a medium oven for 25-30 minutes finishing as above with the cheese.

Avocado and lemon pasta
(Pasta com limao e avocado) Serves 4

225g/8oz large pasta shells (or short-cut pasta like macaroni)
salt, pepper
oil and vinegar dressing
1 large avocado
juice and grated rind of 1 lemon

1 crushed garlic clove
10ml/2 teaspoons sugar
45-60ml/3-4 tablespoons stock or milk
4 chopped spring onions
30ml/2 tablespoons chopped parsley

Cook pasta shells in boiling salted water till just tender. Drain well and toss lightly in oil and vinegar dressing while still warm. Halve the avocado, remove the stone and scoop out the flesh. Blend or beat till smooth with lemon juice and rind, salt and pepper, garlic, sugar and stock. Stir in the onions and parsley. Thin the sauce with extra stock or milk if necessary. Stir the avocado and lemon sauce into the pasta and serve.

Vegetable and pasta stir-fry
(Frito de legumes e pasta) Serves 4

450g/1lb pasta shells (or
  other short-cut pasta)
1 large peeled and sliced
  onion
3 sticks celery cut in strips
2 large carrots, peeled and
  cut in strips
75g/3oz green beans,
  topped and tailed

½ sliced red pepper
½ sliced green pepper
75g/3oz butter
30ml/2 tablespoons soy
  sauce
75g/3oz grated cheese
  (optional)

Boil the pasta in plenty of boiling salted water until tender or
al dente. Drain and refresh under cold water. Melt the butter
and add all the vegetables; use a non-stick pan or wok if
available. Fry gently for about 10 minutes, stirring often till
softened. Add the well-drained pasta and soy sauce. Mix with
the vegetables and cook for a further 2 minutes to heat the
pasta through. Season well and serve with grated cheese
sprinkled on top if wished.

Portuguese risotto
(Arroz a Portuguesa) Serves 4

1 chopped onion
1 green pepper cut in thin
  strips
1 red pepper cut in thin
  strips
45ml/3 tablespoons
  vegetable oil
350g/12oz long-grain rice

2 peeled and chopped
  tomatoes
¾ litre/1½ pints hot stock
1 sliced smoked sausage
  (omit if vegetarian)
vegetable or olive oil or
  butter

Fry the onion and peppers for 3-4 minutes in oil. Add the
tomatoes and rice and fry for 1-2 minutes stirring with a
wooden spoon. Add the hot stock. Bring to the boil and stir
once. Lower heat to simmer, cover the pan and cook for 15
minutes or till the rice is tender and the liquid has been
absorbed. Add the sausage if used, separately browned in oil
or butter. Cover and cook for a further 5 minutes.

Marinated mushrooms with orange
(Salada de cogumelos com laranja) Serves 4

30ml/2 tablespoons
  vegetable oil
150ml/¹⁄₄ pint white wine
2 bay leaves
8 coriander seeds

1 orange
salt, pepper
450g/1lb button
  mushrooms, wiped clean
chopped fresh parsley

Put into a saucepan the oil, wine, bay leaves, coriander, grated rind from the orange and seasoning. Bring to the boil. Cover and simmer for 3 minutes. Add the mushrooms. Cover and simmer for 5 minutes, stirring occasionally. Remove the mushrooms to a bowl, then strain cooking liquor over them. Remove orange peel and cut flesh into slices. Stir into mushrooms, cover and chill. Sprinkle with parsley before serving.

Broad beans are a popular vegetable in Portugal along with peas and these can either be puréed and served on their own or with softly poached eggs on top for a vegetarian or light diet meal.

Broad bean brunch
(Favas com ovos) Serves 3

450/1lb shelled broad beans
¹⁄₄ small lettuce
1 small chopped onion
olive oil

small bunch of fresh
  coriander
eggs for poaching (optional)

Boil beans with chopped lettuce in a very little water. Drain (keep the cooking water). Cool. Skin the broad beans, purée or liquidise with the lettuce. Cook chopped onion in olive oil slowly with the chopped coriander. Cook to a deep golden brown and add to the bean purée with some of the cooking water if necessary. Stir to heat through and serve alone or topped with a poached egg.

For dieters, salads are an easy summer way of eating, especially on holiday. The dressing, however, is what adds the pounds! These three dressing suggestions are low-calorie and easy to make with local ingredients.

Cucumber dressing Serves 2-4
(total calories 257)

Mix 150ml/¼ pint low-calorie natural yoghurt with 30ml/2 tablespoons grated cucumber. Season to taste. This goes well on tomato salad or as a meal starter dip with pieces of raw vegetable.

Honey and vinegar
(total calories 62)

Place 15ml/1 tablespoon clear honey, 150ml/¼ pint vinegar and 2.5ml/½ teaspoon salt, a pinch of black pepper and 5ml/1 teaspoon freshly chopped chives in a screw-topped jar. Shake well and use as needed on salads.

Tomato juice dressing
(total calories 20)

Place 150ml/¼ pint tomato juice, 7½ml/½ tablespoon tarragon vinegar, 1 small crushed garlic clove (optional), salt and black pepper in a screw-topped jar. Chill and shake well before use. This goes well over a mixed salad.

Those with delicate digestions or who need light nourishing food (perhaps after over-indulgence in local wines and putting too much ice in drinks) can have Portuguese old-style chicken soup thickened with rice and enriched if wished with a little smoked ham.

Portuguese chicken soup

1 boiling chicken	parsley
1 portion Lamego or Chaves smoked ham	125g/4oz rice
	1 egg-yolk
2 large onions	

Boil the chicken with the ham, chopped onions and parsley in water to cover for 3-5 hours according to the toughness of the chicken (or use chicken joints if preferred). Top up water as necessary to make a good broth. Add uncooked rice and boil for a further 20 minutes. Mix an egg-yolk with a little of the broth and return to the soup to improve the colour and flavour. Do not reboil after adding the egg.

The following recipe comes from Michel Costa and is intended to be made in the 'catavap' (see page 62) which he invented, but an ordinary steamer can be used instead. The idea is to keep the meat light and tender for an easily digested meal.

Steamed chicken with honey vinegar
(Frango cozido em vapor com vinaigre doce)
Serves 2

¾kg/1½lb chicken
1 medium carrot
2 turnips
2 small leeks
12 mushrooms
1 lemon
1 small courgette
2 dessert spoons wine
   vinegar

5ml/1 teaspoon honey
25g/1oz butter
4 soup spoons fresh cream
12 leaves spinach
small bunch watercress
10 fresh mint leaves
salt, pepper

Wash all the vegetables and peel as necessary. Cut to strips the size of large chips. Wash the mushrooms and sprinkle with the juice of a lemon. Remove the green parts of the leeks and cut the white parts in lengthways strips. Wash spinach, watercress leaves and mint and cut in thin sticks. Put water in the bottom of the 'catavap' or steamer and place chicken and vegetables on the steamer plate. Cover with the lid and cook on a high heat for 14 minutes. Put butter on a low heat in a frying pan and fry the chicken cut in four joints till golden in colour. Drain the butter off and add honey and vinegar. Swirl round the pan then remove chicken and keep hot along with the vegetables. Take 3 soup spoonfuls of the cooking liquid and pour it into the frying pan. Add the cream and make a reduction of the sauce to produce a smooth sauce. Add in the spinach, mint and watercress and cook for 1 minute. Serve at once with the sauce over the vegetables and chicken.

Feeding children extra hungry with sea and fresh air-sharpened appetites needs forethought and a well stocked cupboard. These ideas are quick and sustaining, starting with two tuna sandwich variations which use fresh or canned tuna.

Creamed tuna sandwich
(Pao com atum) Serves 2

50g/2oz mushrooms
12g/¹/₂oz butter
1 × 200g/7oz can tuna,
    drained and flaked
10ml/2 teaspoons lemon
    juice

30ml/2 tablespoons single
    or double cream
salt, pepper
4 slices buttered toast

Slice the mushrooms and fry in butter for 2-3 minutes. Add the tuna, lemon juice and cream. Season to taste. Heat till very hot and serve in the toast sandwich.

Tuna toast
(Atum com torrada) Serves 2

2 thick slices brown bread
12g/¹/₂oz butter
1 separated egg
15ml/1 tablespoon thick
    mayonnaise

87g/3¹/₂oz canned tuna,
    drained and flaked
2¹/₂ml/¹/₂ teaspoon lemon
    juice
salt, pepper

Toast the bread and spread with butter. Whisk the egg-yolk with the mayonnaise till creamy. Beat the egg-white till just stiff. Stir tuna, lemon juice, salt, pepper and 15ml/1 table-spoon egg-white into the egg-yolk and mayonnaise. Fold in the rest of the egg-white. Pile the mixture on the toast and grill under a low heat for 10-12 minutes till set. Serve at once.

Crunchy omelette
(Omeleta com pao) Serves 2

A thrifty way of using up bread and vegetables. This is also suitable for vegetarians.

50g/2oz butter or margarine
2 large slices bread (crusts
    removed and cut in 1cm/
    1¹/₂-inch cubes)

2 small sliced onions
125g/4oz sliced mushrooms
4 beaten eggs
salt, pepper

Melt butter in an omelette pan and gently fry the bread and onion for 5-6 minutes till golden brown. Add the mushrooms and cook for 1 minute. Beat the eggs and seasoning and add to the pan, stirring and drawing the mixture from the sides to the centre of the pan, till almost set. Cover the pan and cook until the egg is set and the omelette golden brown underneath. Serve flat. Other vegetables such as chopped tomato, green pepper or spring onions can be used and any chopped, cooked vegetable can be included in the mixture.

Many children have a seemingly in-built resistance to rice as a pudding but this vanilla or lemon-flavoured creamy rice made the Portuguese way is perfect for children and those with delicate digestions.

Sweet rice
(Arroz doce) Serves 3-4

To 1 cup rice add 2 cups milk and boil slowly together with lemon peel or a vanilla stick. When the rice is well cooked, gradually stir in 2-3 beaten egg-yolks. Continue to stir till the mixture thickens. Do not allow to boil after the eggs have been added. Pour the mixture onto a large, flat dish. Remove vanilla stick and allow it to get cold. Then serve sprinkled with cinnamon.

Rabanadas is an easy idea that transforms stale bread into a treat for small children and is much loved by the Portuguese young in the north. Soak slices of cold toast in a mixture of sugar, milk and beaten egg. Fry the bread in oil. Make a syrup from sugar and water (boil 225g/8oz sugar and 275ml/$\frac{1}{2}$ pint water till dark and syrupy). Pour the syrup over the bread slices and serve hot or cold.

For a small child's tea, a similar idea to the sweet syrupy *rabanadas* is *pao constipado* (bread with a cold) from the southern part of Portugal, the Algarve. Fry slices of bread in olive oil. Remove from the pan and dip fairly quickly in cold water. Drain excess water off and coat bread with sugar and powdered cinnamon.

Another quick sweet pudding or snack using bananas and lemon juice is the following one.

Fried banana sandwich
(Sandwiche de banana frite) Makes 4

*8 medium-thick slices of
  bread
butter to spread
2 bananas*

*lemon juice
15ml/1 tablespoon white or
  brown sugar*

Remove the crusts from the bread and spread with butter.
Mash bananas with lemon juice and sugar to taste. Use as a
sandwich filling. Spread the outside of the sandwiches with
butter and fry over a low heat, turning once for about 5
minutes till golden brown on both sides. Jam or lemon curd
can be substituted for the banana.

12
EATING
OUT

Since the 1970s the cooking of traditional Portuguese food has shifted away from homes to restaurants. Antonio Penha of the Lisbon hotel school told me that in the past 7-8 years, women have even given up becoming chefs, whereas in the past there was a great tradition of this. Younger women no longer know the old recipes and serve more convenience foods than in the past and also have more interest in health food and weight-watching. Their mothers have lost the services of maids and cooks, customary in many households before the revolution of the 1970s, and with them went many of the domestic recipe secrets. Recently, however, there have been a number of excellent traditional recipe books published in Portugal which should do much towards preventing the entire loss of cooking culture.

Portugal's abundant restaurants preserve tradition all over the country. The larger hotels and some restaurants will serve a more international menu and Chinese restaurants are fairly prevalent, though not as popular as once they were.

The Portuguese love their food and this is evident in the care and attention they give to it, discussing dishes at length with restaurant waiters and proprietors. On the whole, while restaurants are clean and neat, they do not go for elaborate decors and lengthy menus. The food quality is more important than the setting. Often the best meals are found in very modest-looking *pensaos* in the countryside or tiny single rooms in the cities, such as the Bairro Alto area in Lisbon where there are dozens of small restaurants. One may find oneself rubbing shoulders with a fisherman or wealthy banker, watched anxiously by waiters to make sure the food pleases. Primavera, Travessa Espera 34 in Lisbon, is one such place that has survived many years. In fact it is comforting to know that many of the restaurants I knew in the late 1960s and early 1970s are still flourishing. In Lisbon, Varinha da Madragoa, Rua Madres 36, in the narrow streeted Madragoa area of art galleries, is set behind a red wood door that looks firmly shut, has white tiled walls, gingham cloths and candles, serves five kinds of cod and three kinds of steak. A meal here will cost about 500-600 *escudos*.

The restaurants, too, with exceptions in more popular areas, remain characterful and untouristy, but use local craftware. Paper table-top covers are often found in restaurants, renewed for each customer, and food is often served in the common thick brown earthenware dishes; house wine comes in a brown earthenware jug. The portions are always more than ample and second helpings are happily brought from the large platters and pots. The custom of listing $\frac{1}{2}$ 'doses' (portions) on menus still exists though quality is now more of a concern than quantity. The habit is most persistent in the north, in Oporto, where appetites are bigger.

Nouvelle cuisine is not really in the Portuguese eating character, but in Lisbon one or two chefs are making a reputation for themselves on this theme. One is Michel Costa, half-French, half Portuguese, with his restaurant at Largo de Santa Cruz do Castelo 5. Here Portuguese-based dishes are given nouvelle cuisine presentation styles. A signature note is to put vegetables and sauces on the plates in red, white and green combinations — the colours of the Portuguese flag. Puréed brussel sprouts and carrots, for example, go with veal. Michel makes his own port, raspberry and honey vinegars and mustards and serves an unusual hors d'oeuvres salad combining lettuce, cheese, mushrooms, and mussels in vinegar with banana and orange slices placed around the lettuce mixture.

I have mentioned the delightful way waiters serve oranges, peeled and fanned out in segments and slices. This juicy fruit makes a year-round palate cleanser in restaurants. But even in busy restaurants waiters will take fish off the bone and bring back second portions kept hot in the kitchen.

For eating out, Portugal is one of the cheapest of European countries. Thomas Cook runs a regular survey of cost-of-living indexes in top holiday countries and Portugal comes out cheapest of a dozen places for dinner and wine costs, cups of coffee, soft drinks and beer.

Current figures issued by the Portuguese Tourist Office give average restaurant prices as from 1700-3800 *escudos* in a de luxe restaurant for three courses, coffee and half bottle of good table wine. In a first-class restaurant, the price would be 1400-2200 *escudos*; in a second-class restaurant 380-900 *escudos* and also at a tasca or third-class restaurant; and 500-700 *escudos* in a coffee-shop. An ice cream costs from 50 *escudos* and a hamburger is 65-150 *escudos*.

One can, of course, pay more at Tavares, one of Lisbon's top luxury restaurants, where a meal for two with wine will be about 8000 *escudos*. In Lisbon meals in an average second-class restaurant with wine will be about 700 *escudos*. In the Algarve, the most tourist-filled area, it will rise to about 1000 *escudos*.

In Portugal one has a variety of types of restaurants from which to choose. There are guides to help, such as *A Guide to the Best Restaurants in Portugal* (in English but published in Portugal), which also gives useful notes on wines and regional foods. The tourist office will help with lists and information. It has encouraged the use of traditional recipes in restaurants, with annual competitions. In Viana, in the north, the tourist office is producing a list of local chefs and restaurants.

The hotels may be more orientated to international visitor tastes but still serve Portuguese dishes. One can, for example, eat in the Lisbon Sheraton's Alfama Grill off *bacalhau* and *cataplana* recipes and the Lisbon soup *Ameijoas a Bulhao Pato*, clam broth with herbs and garlic (named for a poet); or an *açorda de marisco*, a bread, seafood, egg and fresh coriander fish dish; or *frango na pucara*, chicken in the pot, a good country-style dish. The Albatroz at Cascais, amid its elegant decor overlooking the sea, will also serve *bacalhau*, spit roasted squid, pork with clams in the Alentejo style, roast kid, clams in the *cataplana*, as well as international dishes.

More characteristic of the country are the *estalagems* and *pousadas* for both accommodation and eating. *Estalagems* are inns and can be in new or ancient buildings, private or state-owned, but must always have a restaurant. Examples around Lisbon can range from the newly-opened (in an old private house) Estalagem Senora da Guia near Cascais, overlooking the sea, where the dining room is in country style in the basement and serves a simple menu of codfish with cream sauce and sweet egg pudding type of recipes.

Pousadas were originally set up before World War II by the government to provide accommodation in remoter regions which were historically or scenically of interest to encourage the motoring tourist. Then limits of five-night stays were imposed to encourage people to keep moving along, but now this restriction has been lifted, though the word *pousada* means to 'perch'. The management has changed from franchise to government employee. There are currently about 27 *pousadas* in mainland Portugal, in all parts of the country, housed in a variety of buildings most of which are architectural and historical gems. A new one is opening at Guimares this year.

My favourite *pousadas* include the S. Teotonio at Valenca, snugged into a huge, walled rampart overlooking the river border with Spain in the very north of the country; and the *castelo* at Obidos, north of Lisbon, looking down over the little white-washed Moorish town, traditionally the honeymoon present of the kings of Portugal to their queens; the castle at Palmela, south of Lisbon; the Santa Isabel at Estremoz, in a former queen's home; and the countrified Sao Bras at Alportel in the Algarve above Faro. This last has sunny views down over the almond and orange groves towards the sea and a lovely kitchen decorated with old plates. There is a second *pousada* in the Algarve, the Infante at Sagres, where the seafood is excellent.

It is a pleasant way of seeing Portugal to tour staying at the *pousadas* and the tourist board has a leaflet with suggested routes. But if there is a *pousada* near you, it is well worth a visit for an authentic meal in typical local style. For example, in the ducal setting of a castle at Palmela, each day a Portuguese speciality menu is suggested, as at all *pousadas*. The visitor has the choice of menus at two price levels according to the number of courses. For four courses the price is 1750 *escudos*. At Palmela, the rich and sweet recipes of the old convents are used to fill the sweet trolley: purées of egg-yolks, *chila* (pumpkin), potato or bread scattered with cinnamon that are delicious in spite of the sound of the ingredients. A *toucinho* recipe of caramel custard has bacon in it to give it a remarkably rich taste and colour.

A new kind of accommodation is opening up — the private manor houses which offer rooms to visitors. Some have self-catering apartments or cottages to let. Most do not offer more than breakfast but a few will welcome visitors for meals if a phone booking is made. One such place is the English-owned Quinta Sao Thiago, down narrow lanes beyond Sintra, where a dinner at the long refectory table of five courses is from 2400-3000 *escudos*. It will include some Portuguese-style dishes made from fresh daily produce.

Of the restaurant types, apart from the evening *fado* houses where Portuguese food is usually served, the simple ones in *pensaos* or third-class restaurants give superb value and usually good food. Near the sea one can be fairly confident that the fish will be excellent and fresh unless it is an extremely touristy spot. For sole, the restaurants at Cacil-has, across the Tagus from Lisbon, are the places to go, especially to Floresta do Ginjal, the entrance decorated with hundreds of shells. Around the Nazare area many fisher-men's wives, bored in their husband's absence, set up little restaurants of their own. Many in the south are basic units on the beach with little barbecues to do the cooking.

The *tascas* are third-class restaurants, usually small, very plain, and serving good local food often with a bar for stand-up snacks and drinks. *Tascinhos*, originating in Spain, are smaller style restaurants where *pudim* flan was first sold. *Tasca* may be translated as a tavern. It is popular, with typical small dishes, often based on chicken, meat, kidneys and offal, served with wine or beer. There will be local ham or *pasteis de bacalhau* with beans.

Lugas are tiny general stores found all over the country that persist against the growing number of supermarkets and mini-markets. Many are run by wives who go to the market at 6am each day to buy fresh produce for sale along with dry goods. The market tradition is to upturn a few empty boxes at midday to make a table and seats and then to cook a meal. Lurdes is a lady who does this for friends and privi-leged customers behind her small shop in Lisbon. Few tourists will probably get to eat this way, but if a friendly *luga* owner where you shop invites you, do not pass up the invita-tion even if it is only for good black coffee and a drop of the brandy of the house.

The tea shop (*casa de cha*) may have died out in the UK when emancipation gave ladies other forms of occupation, but it is alive and well all over Portugal along with its parallel, the coffee shop. Though each village will have its tea shop or *pastelaria* where the local sweetmeat is sold (to eat on the spot or take away), Lisbon is particularly fond of its tea and coffee shops where the gossip flows. In the Baixa area the most popular tea rooms are Ferrari, Caravela and Bernard. Vicentinas on Rato square is still run by old ladies.

Coffee rooms are mainly clustered around Rossio square and on the wide black and white mosaiced pavements and central areas of the Avenida da Liberdade, the central road artery of the city, where in summer tables are set out for coffee and snacks.

In the afternoon, tea with thick fingers of hot buttered toast is popular in winter, as well as sweetmeats. But in fact the *casa de cha* provide day-long snacks and light meals to sustain the shopper or sightseer. Tea-rooms are licensed and serve wines, beers and spirits as well as tea and coffee. A light meal — for example, hot toasted sandwiches, fruit and wine — can be taken as required.

There are also many stand-up bars in which to take coffee and coffee in Portugal is delicious, mainly coming from Brazil. There is quite a little dictionary of terms for the coffee-conscious to cultivate in Portugal. *Cafe* comes strong in little cups; *com leite* means with milk (and sugar will be automatically brought). *Bica* is strong coffee in a tiny cup; *espresso* is strong as elsewhere; *garato* (translated 'little boy') is hot milk with strong coffee in a small cup. *Carioca* (also the term for inhabitants of Rio in Brazil) is a mix of hot water and strong coffee served in a glass or bigger cup. *Galao* is strong with hot milk in a tall glass; *galao escuro* a darker version of this, and *galao claro* is a lighter, milkier style also called *pingado*.

Incidentally, asking for lemon tea, one may be served not ordinary tea with a slice of lemon but a ready-mixed, lemon-flavoured infusion which is light and refreshing.

Though the Portuguese are not as passionate snackers as, say, the Dutch, there are opportunities for light meals on the move. In June in Lisbon there are the grilled sardine stalls which also sell glasses of *vinho verde* in the Alfama section streets. At Mealhada, in central Portugal, the speciality is slices of bread with pieces of freshly roasted sucking pig. All over the country in simpler restaurants, a quick, cheap and appetising couple of dishes to ask for when you do not want a full meal are a *bitoque* and a *prego*. *Bitoque* means 'knock twice' and is a thin but juicy steak cooked in an earthenware dish topped with a fried egg and surrounded by fried pota-toes — a Portuguese favourite. A *prego* is sliced beef in a sandwich or on a plate. Often veal is used in this dish and *prego na plate* means a version on a plate served with chips.

The Portuguese eat much nearer to our mealtimes than the Spanish do. Lunch will be 12.30 or 1pm, though some eat at 2pm. Dinner is eaten from 8-9pm usually when eating out, though it is a little earlier in the country areas and at home the TV programmes dictate the time. On public holidays, the evening meal may be taken much later — from 10-11pm. Restaurants (as well as musuems) are often closed on Mondays in Lisbon.

When one sits down at a restaurant table there is always something there to nibble while the menu and wine selection are discussed. There is usually a savoury butter (which one can also buy ready-made at the *pastelaria*) and a basket of crisp slices of toasted bread or crusty soft bread may be brought, and in some cases a small selection of breads, including wholemeal. Little dishes of olives, small pieces of smoked hams, slices of seasonal or local cheeses or paté may also be offered.

In tourist areas, menus will be available in English and many Portuguese speak a little French if the menu translation proves difficult. The menu will break down into soups (*sopa*), including one referred to as *panada*, a bread soup similar to *açorda*, hors d'oeuvres, fish *entree*, meat, and pudding or cheese. Puddings, as earlier remarked, are mainly variations on caramel custards and convent-style dishes with chocolate mousse a close runner-up favourite. Tropical types of fruits from Madeira and the Azores will be offered as available.

Although I have mentioned some regional foods in previous chapters, to guide the traveller in some of the more common foods to expect in restaurants around Portugal, here are a few notes on cuisine region by region.

Alentejo Gazpacho and bread soups; pork and sausages; sheep's milk cheeses; *bacalhau* eaten with rice and coriander; turkey pie; stewed partridge with onion sauce; sweets with lovely names like Nun's Bellies, Priest's ears, Jesuits, and Rotten Cake (*bolo podre*), made with honey, powdered cinnamon, flour and olive oil.

Algarve Corn bread; morcela Algarvia, a local sausage; on the coast, fish dishes; inland more pork is eaten, which can be cooked with squid; *cataplana* dishes with clams and pork; tuna steaks; partridges with clams; Dom Rodrigo sweet.

Beira Alta Trout from the rivers; a poor cuisine with little beef eaten, instead roast goat, cabbage and sprouts as vegetables; hare soup, whiting, trout in onion sauce; stuffed pork belly; new potatoes cooked in their skins then removed and boiled in tomato and onion sauce; apple pudding.

Beira Baixa More meat than fish eaten; dry chestnut soup; garlic-spiced fish soup; eels with bread; meat stews; plums stuffed with nuts.

Beira Litoral Renowned for the length of its sausages; goat in the *chanfana* dish; suckling pig is very typical; eel broth (fishermen's stew); sweet rice; bread pudding; sponge cake.

Estremadura Where Lisbon is situated, so much regional identity has been lost. Fish at Cascais, and Sesimbra; seafood soups, ox-tail soup; duck with olives; broad beans; bean cakes.

Minho One of the richest regional cuisines in Portugal. Goat and lamprey are much eaten. *Caldo verde* soup; dry soup; chicken broth; octopus and *bacalhau* dishes.

Ribatejo A wide variety of river fish is the basis of eating here, along with eggs, fruit and game birds. Also mullet, eels, hare stew, broad beans with yellow sauce, goat cutlets, carrot pudding.

Tras os Montes The principal meat here is pork, smoked or salted, with home-made sausages; trout, sardines and codfish. Chestnuts go with meat dishes, though potatoes and cabbage are also used. *Douro* dry soup, cooked in the oven with cabbage and smoked ham; bean soup; sardine pie; meat pie; rabbit; dessert golden soup with bread, egg-yolks and sugar; nougat.

Glossary of Portuguese Words and Phrases

GENERAL PHRASES

Greetings

good morning	*bom dia*
good afternoon or evening	*boa tarde*
goodnight	*boa noite*
goodbye	*adeus*
cheers	*saúde*
yes	*sim*
no	*não*
please	*por favor*
I am sorry	*desculpe*
I want	*enquero*
I don't understand	*não compreendo*
how much is it?	*quanto custa?*
please	*se fáz favor*
please call me a taxi	*chame me um taxi por favor*
please help me	*ajude me por favor*
please tell me	*informe-me por favor*
thank you	*obrigada* (when said by a woman); *obrigado* (when said by a man)
where?	*onde?*
why?	*porquê?*
where is?	*onde é?*
where is (of a place)?	*onde fica?*
I am	*tenho*
thirsty	*sede*
hungry	*fome*
in a hurry	*pressa*

117

Days, Months, Seasons

Sunday	*Domingo*
Monday	*Segunda-feira*
Tuesday	*Terca-feira*
Wednesday	*Quarta-feira*
Thursday	*Quinta-feira*
Friday	*Sexta-feira*
Saturday	*Sábado*
January	*Janeiro*
February	*Fevereiro*
March	*Marco*
April	*Abril*
May	*Maio*
June	*Junho*
July	*Julho*
August	*Agosto*
September	*Setembro*
October	*Outubro*
November	*Novembro*
December	*Dezembro*
Spring	*primavera*
Summer	*verao*
Autumn	*outono*
Winter	*inverno*

Numerals

one	*um*
two	*dois*
three	*três*
four	*quatro*
five	*cinco*
six	*seis*
seven	*sete*
eight	*oito*
nine	*nove*
ten	*dez*
eleven	*onze*
twelve	*doze*
thirteen	*treze*
fourteen	*catorze*
fifteen	*quinze*
sixteen	*dezasseis*
seventeen	*dezassete*
eighteen	*dezoito*
nineteen	*dezanove*

twenty	*vinte*
thirty	*trinta*
forty	*quarenta*
fifty	*cinquenta*
sixty	*sessenta*
seventy	*setenta*
eighty	*oitenta*
ninety	*noventa*
one hundred	*cem*
one thousand	*mil*

Time

what time is it?	*que horas são?*
when?	*quando*
do you open?	*abrem?*
shut?	*fecham?*
when will it be ready?	*quando fica pronto?*
very soon	*logo*
tomorrow	*amanhã*
today	*hoje*
this afternoon	*logo à tarde*
this evening	*logo à noite*
yesterday	*ontem*
late	*tarde*
early	*cedo*
one day	*um dia*
one night	*uma noite*
midday	*meio dia*
midnight	*meia noite*

Measurements

big	*grande*
bigger	*maior*
small	*pequeno*
smaller	*mais pequeno*
wide	*largo*
tight	*apertado*
long	*comprido*
short	*curto*
round	*redondo*
square	*quadrado*
thick	*espesso*
thin	*fino*

Colours

black	*preto*
blue	*azul*
brown	*castanho*
dark	*escuro*
green	*verde*
grey	*cinzento*
light	*claro*
pink	*cor de rosa*
red	*encarnado*
white	*branco*
yellow	*amarelo*

Shopping

bakers	*padaria*
butchers	*talho*
cheap	*barato*
crafts shop	*artesanato*
expensive	*caro*
fishmongers	*peixaria*
grocers	*mercearia*
jewellers	*joalaria*
market	*mercado*
pastry shop	*pastelaria*
pound (weight)	*meio quilo*
shoe shop	*sapataria*
souvenirs	*lembranças*
stationers	*papelaria*
supermarket	*supermercado*

Toilets

gents	*cavalheiros/homens*
ladies	*senhoras*
engaged	*ocupado*
vacant	*livre*

FOOD AND CULINARY TERMS

Ways of Cooking

baked	*no forno*
boiled	*cozido* (of eggs)
braised	*nas brasas* (on charcoal grill)
bread-crumbed (and fried)	*panada/o*
browned	*corado*
chop	*costoleta*
cocotte	*em cocotte*

croquette	*croquete*
fried	*frito*
grilled	*grelhado*
just done	*médio*
mashed	*puré*
medium	*médio*
minced	*moido/a* (or *passado* applied to meat)
pie	*empada*
rare	*mal passado*
raw	*cru*
roasted	*corado/assado*
rolled	*enrolado*
salted	*salgado/a*
sauté	*salteado*
smoked	*fumado*
soft	*tenro mole*
spit-roasted	*no espeto*
steamed	*cozido a vapor*
stewed	*guisado*
thick	*espesso*
well done	*bem passado*

Ways of Preparing Eggs

boiled	*quentes*
fried	*estrelados*
hard-boiled	*cozidos*
omelette	*omeleta*
poached	*escalfados*
scrambled	*mexidos*

Fish

anchovies	*anchovas*
bass	*robalo*
bream	*pargo*
brill	*mero*
carp	*carpa*
cod	*bacalhau*
eels	*eirós/enguia*
grey mullet	*mugem*
grouper	*cherne*
hake	*pescada*
herring	*arenque*
mackerel	*carapau*
plaice	*solha*
red mullet	*salmonete*

sardines	*sardinhas*
scabbard fish	*peixe espada*
sea bass	*robalo*
sea eel	*eiróz*
shad	*savel*
skate	*raia*
sole	*linguado*
swordfish	*espadarte*
trout	*truta*
tuna	*atum*
turbot	*rodovalho*
whiting	*pescadinha*

Shellfish

barnacles	*perceves*
cockles	*ameijoas*
crabs	*caranguejos* (big crabs, *santola*)
crayfish	*lagostins*
cuttlefish	*chocos*
lobster	*lagosta*
mussels	*mexilhœs*
octopus	*polvo*
oysters	*ostras*
prawns	*gambas*
scallops	*vieiras*
shrimps	*camarœs*
squid	*lulas*

Poultry and Game

boar	*javali*
cock	*galo*
chicken	*frango*
duck	*pato* (wild duck, *pato bravo*)
goose	*ganso*
hare	*lebre*
hen	*galinha*
partridge	*perdiz*
pheasant	*faisão*
pigeon	*pombo*
quail	*codorniz*
rabbit	*coelho*
turkey	*perú*
venison	*veado*
woodcock	*galinhola*

Meat

bacon	*bacon*
beef	*carne de vaca*
beefburger	*bife de carne picada*
brains	*mioleira*
escalope	*escalope*
fillet	*lombo*
ham	*fiambre*
hot dog	*cachorro*
kid	*cabrito*
kidneys	*rins*
lamb	*anho/borrego*
liver	fígado (*iscas* when cooked)
mutton	*carneiro*
oxtail	*rabo de vaca*
pork	*porco*
rumpsteak	*entrecote*
sausage	*salsicha*
smoked ham	*presunto*
spare ribs	*entrecosto*
steak	*bife*
suckling pig	*leitão*
tongue	*lingua*
tripe	*dobrada*
veal	*vitela*

Meat Cuts

breast	*peito*
chop, cutlet	*costoleta*
entrecote	*entrecosto*
escalope	*escalope*
fillet	*filetes*
leg	*perna*
loin	*lombo*
mince	*carne picada*
neck	*cachaco/pescoço*
shoulder	*pá*
steak	*bife*
stewing meat	*carne para guisar*
tournedos steak	*tornedos*

Fruit and Nuts

almonds	*amendoas*
apple	*macã*
apricots	*alperces*

avocados	*pêra abacate*
bananas	*bananas*
cherry	*cereja*
chestnut	*castanhas*
figs	*figos*
grapefruit	*toranja*
grapes	*uvas*
hazelnuts	*avelãs*
lemon	*limão*
lime	*lima*
medlars	*nêsperas*
melon	*melão*
orange	*laranja*
papaya	*papaia*
peach	*pessego*
peanuts	*amendoim*
pear	*pêra*
pineapple	*ananás*
plums	*ameixas*
pomegranates	*romãs*
raspberries	*framboesas*
strawberries	*morangos* (wild, *morangos-silvestres*)
tangerine	*tangerinas*
walnut	*noz*
water-melon	*melância*

Vegetables

artichokes	*alcachofras*
asparagus	*aspargos*
aubergine	*beringelas*
beans	*feijão*
beetroot	*beterraba*
broad beans	*favas*
broccoli	*broculos*
Brussels sprouts	*couve de bruxelas*
cabbage	*couve*
carrots	*cenouras*
cauliflower	*couve flor*
celery	*aipo*
cucumber	*pepino*
French beans	*feijão verde*
garlic	*alho*
gherkins	*pepinos pequenos*
leek	*alho porro*
lettuce	*alface*

mushrooms	*cogumelos*
olives	*azeitonas* (black, *pretas*; stuffed, *recheadas*; green, *verde*)
onions	*cebolas*
parsley	*salsa*
parsnip	*pastinaca*
peas	*ervilhas*
peppers	*pimentos*
potatoes	*batatas*
pumpkin	*abobora/chila*
radishes	*rabanetes*
spinach	*espinafres*
tomato	*tomate*
turnips	*nabos*
watercress	*agriœs*
white beans	*feijão branco*

Meals

breakfast	*pequeno almoço*
lunch	*almoço*
dinner	*jantar*
tea	*lanche*
menu	*ementa*
hors d'oeuvres	*acepipes*
course/dish	*prato*
soups	*sopas*

Eating Out

ashtray	*cinzeiro*
bar	*bar*
bill	*conta*
bottle (of wine)	*garrafa*
half-bottle	*meia garrafa*
carafe	*jarro de vinho*
cloakroom	*vestiário/bengaleiro*
chair	*cadeira*
cup	*chávena*
dessert	*sobremesa*
finger-bowl	*taca para os dedos*
fork	*garfo*
glass	*copo*
ice-cream	*gelado*
jug of water	*jarro de agua*
knife	*faca*
napkin	*guardanapa*

peppermill	*moinho a para a pimenta*
plate	*prato*
restaurant	*restaurante*
sandwich	*sande/sandwiche* (toasted, *tosta*)
small	*pequeno*
spoon	*colher*
sweets	*doces*
table	*mesa*
terrace	*terraco*
tip	*gorjeta*
toothpick	*palito*
vegetarian	*vegetariano*
waiter	*empregado de mesa* (when calling for: *criado*/waitress-*criada*)
head waiter	*chefe de mesa*
wine-list	*lista/carta de vinhos*
with	*com*
without	*sem*

Groceries, Dry Goods, Supermarkets

biscuit	*biscoito*
butter	*manteiga*
bread	*pão*, rolls *paezinhos*; wholemeal *pão escuro/pão integral*
cake	*bolo*
cheese	*queijo*
chocolate	*chocolate*
cigarettes	*cigarros*
cigars	*charutos*
cream	*natas*
eggs	*ovas*
fat (grease)	*gordura*
flour	*farinha*
fruit juice	*sumo de fruta*
honey	*mel*
ice-cream	*gelado*
jam	*conserva/compota*
ketchup	*molho ketchup*
lard	*banha*
lentils	*lentilhas*
macaroni	*macarrao*
marmalade	*maramelada* (quince jelly)

matches	*fósfẽros*
mayonnaise	*maionese*
mustard	*mostarda*
oil	*óleo*
pastries	*pasteis*
pastry (dough)	*massa*
pepper	*pimenta*
pipe tobacco	*tabaco para cachimbo*
raisin	*passa*
rice	*arroz*
saccharine	*sacarina*
salt	*sal*
sauce	*molho*
soap	*sabonete*
spaghetti	*esparguete*
sponge cake	*pão de ló*
sugar	*açúcar* (granulated, *granulado*)
toast	*torradas*
toilet paper	*papel higiénico*
vinegar	*vinagre*

Herbs and Spices

anise	*anis*
basil	*basilico*
caraway	*alcaravia*
chervil	*cerefólio*
chilli pepper	*malagueta*
chives	*cebolinha filamentos*
cinnamon	*canela*
clove	*cravo da India*
coriander	*coentro*
cumin	*cominho*
curry	*caril*
garlic	*alho*
ginger	*gengibre*
marjoram	*mangerona*
mint	*hortelã*
nutmeg	*nóz moscada*
parsley	*salsa*
rosemary	*rosmaninho*
saffron	*açafrão*
sage	*salva*
sorrel	*azedinha*
spice	*especiaria/condimento*
tarragon	*estragão*

thyme	*tomilho*
vanilla	*baunilha*

Drinks

beer	*cerveja* (dark beer, *preta*)
bitter	*amargo*
brandy (local)	*aguardente* (cognac, *conhaque*)
champagne	*champanhe*
chocolate (hot)	*chocolate quente*
cider	*cidra*
cocoa	*cacau*
coffee	*café* (with milk, *cafe com leite*; caffein-free, *sem cafeina*; weak, *carioca*)
dry	*seco*
gin	*gin*
juices	*sumos*
lemonade	*limonada*
liqueur	*licor*
milk	*leite*
milk-shake	*batido*
mineral water	*agua mineral*
orangeade	*laranjada*
soda water	*agua gasosa de soda*
soft drink	*bebida não alcoólica*
sweet	*doce*
tea	*cha* (iced tea with lemon, *chá gelado com limão*)
rum	*ron, rum*
water	*agua* (drinking water, *agua potável*)
wines	*vinhos*
red	*vinho tinto*
rose	*rosé*
white	*vinho branco*
house wine	*vinho da casa*
local wine	*vinho da região*
table wine	*vinho de mesa*
young wine	*vinho verde*

Bibliography

GUIDE BOOKS AND MAPS

Baedeker Portugal (distributed by the AA)
Touring Map of Portugal (distributed by the AA)
Country Map of Spain and Portugal (Collins)
Touring Map of Portugal (Collins)
The Blue Guide to Portugal, Ian Roberston (A. & C. Black)
Traveller's Portugal, Anthony Hogg (Solo Mio) Tours for
   Motorists
The Rough Guide to Portugal, Mark Ellingham and John
   Fisher (Routledge)
Berlitz Guide to Lisbon (Cassell)
Berlitz Guide to the Algarve (Cassell)
Michelin Guide to España and Portugal

OLDER BOOKS

 (mostly out of print but worth looking for):
They Went to Portugal, Rose Macaulay (Cape)
The Wine of Portugal, Jan Read (Faber, 1982)
Portuguese Wine, Raymond Postgate (Dent)
The Cooking of Spain and Portugal, Peter S. Feibleman
   (Time-Life Foods of the World series)
Portuguese Food, Carol Wright (Dent)
Lisbon, Carol Wright (Dent)

Index

131